N.A.I.L.E.D.

THE ULTIMATE GUIDE TO GET YOUR DREAM TECH JOB

Interviewers at Google, Meta, TikTok, and Salesforce share their tips and tricks to ace any tech interview (including some of the most common interview questions with detailed answers)

MATTEO TONARELLI & PILAR ALFONSO RICO

INDEX

Welcome to N.A.I.L.E.D., a transformative guide designed to be your compass in the ever-changing career development landscape. In an era where the job market is more competitive than ever, we recognize the need for a comprehensive approach that goes far beyond the traditional boundaries of career advice.

In the first chapters, we will provide you with unique insider insights into the lives of tech employees to help guide your career choices. We believe in the importance of making informed choices. The decisions you make today shape the trajectory of your professional future. Whether you are a recent graduate starting your career journey or a professional seeking a change, *N.A.I.L.E.D.* is crafted to provide you with all the insights needed to make essential career choices with a more educated approach.

Then, in chapter 8, we dive into the nitty gritty of our methodology to help you NAIL any interview. Preparation is your greatest asset in an unpredictable job market. From a compelling résumé to clear frameworks to tackle any interview question, we guide you through the essential readiness elements. We believe that interview preparation is a "field of knowledge" on its own, meaning this subject can be studied and analyzed to develop statistically proven strategies to help increase the average chances of success. We created the N.A.I.L.E.D. methodology after years of working as interviewers at Google (Matteo was Senior Business Development Manager and Head of New Business Iberia for 5 years and completed 160 interviews in these roles; then EMEA Manager for Partners Operations at YouTube for another 2.5 years, completing 150 interviews), TikTok

(Pilar has been the Head of Startups Iberia at TikTok since 2021, she has already carried out more than 180 interviews to build her team), Meta (where Pilar was Client Solution Manager for three years carrying out 40 interviews), and Salesforce (where Matteo was Regional Vice President for the Southern Europe ECS Public Sector for two years, carrying out 220 interviews to build his team from scratch) and after interviewing more than thirty hiring managers and recruiters at top tech corporations and scale-ups. The N.A.I.L.E.D. methodology isn't just a framework; it's a whole mindset that will position you as a formidable contender in any professional arena, based on over thirty years of combined experience as tech professionals.

We have added a few stories of resilience and adaptability that help illustrate that success is not reserved for a selected few but for those who dare to embrace change and innovation.

In the following pages, we invite you to embark on a journey of self-discovery, strategic decision-making, and interview mastery. May the pages ahead serve as a guide and a companion, offering the support we wished we had during our formative years. We hope you find inspiration, clarity, and the tools needed to help your career resonate with your biggest aspirations.

PART 1.

LIFE DECISIONS...

Introduction

YOUR PATHWAY
TO CAREER SUCCESS

"I feel there's an existential angst among young people.
I didn't have that. They see enormous mountains,
where I only saw one little hill to climb."
—*Sergey Brin, co-founder of Google/Alphabet.*

Here are a few interest fact about Sergey Brin[1]:

- Brin's mother was a NASA scientist, and his father was a mathematician.

- He earned a bachelor's degree in mathematics and computer science and then signed up for a PhD in computer science at Stanford University. This decision changed his life.

- While studying for his PhD, Sergey met Larry Page (the other co-founder of Google) in 1995. Together, they launched the first search engine called BackRub. It operated on Stanford servers throughout 1996 until it began to take up too much bandwidth. In 1997, Sergey and Larry renamed their search engine after a play on the word "googol." This equals the number one, followed by 100 zeroes. Thus, Google became a name that meant the endless possibility of information.

---

1 Malseed, M. (February 2007). "The Story of Sergey Brin".

- Google was developed in the garage of Susan Wojcicki, current YouTube CEO, with a $1M startup investment from private donors.

- In 2004, Sergey Brin became the youngest person in the Forbes 400 list of wealthiest people in the world. As of 2024, Sergei's net worth is $124B[2].

- Sergey Brin returned to an active role in Alphabet's operations in 2023, focusing particularly on the development of Google's latest artificial intelligence system, Gemini.

A party for 3,000 people in a privately rented theme park. An all-paid ski trip for one week in Kitzbuhel, Austria. A private concert with guest stars such as Rihanna and Jay-Z in Los Angeles. These are just some fantastic experiences we have had while working for companies such as Google, Meta, and Salesforce. On top of these incredible moments and lifetime friends, these companies taught us the skills, branded us, and gave us the network needed to boost our careers and become financially independent. Of course, it wasn't all glitter and parties. Having a career in these companies requires hard work and dedication. Nonetheless, we do believe that anyone motivated enough could be successful in getting a job at these highly prestigious tech companies (keep in mind that, a few exceptions aside, most of these companies are open to hiring people who hold no degrees as long as they ace the numerous rounds of interviews). **The real problem is how to get in.**

In 2019, Google alone received more than 3,000,000 CVs. Only 0.67% of applicants got a job[3]. At the time of writing, most tech companies are going through a hiring freeze or executing rounds of mass layoffs. Getting a job within these big corporations has become

2 "Forbes' Real-Time Billionaires List: Sergey Brin". *Forbes*. Retrieved March 20, 2024.

3 Popomaronus, T. (2019, April 17). *Here's how many google interviews it takes to hire a googler.* CNBC. https://www.cnbc.com/2019/04/17/heres-how-many-google-job-interviews-it-takes-to-hire-a-googler.html

more complex than ever. That's why getting insider tips on what an interview entails and how to prepare best is crucial to come out on top of the competition and maximize your chances of success.

Having conducted almost 1,000 interviews ourselves and using insight from our network of friends and colleagues working for the most important tech companies in the world, we decided with Pilar to gather exclusive and unique content of an insider's view on how interviews are conducted within these companies and how to best prepare for them.

While each tech company has its interview process and an infinite number of questions that candidates might be asked, tech companies are all looking for very similar sets of skills and personalities. So, the interview format and, most importantly, the interviewers' expectations are very similar from one company to the next.

In the following pages, we plan to share these expectations and how to prepare to ace any tech interview. We've curated a list of the 100 most common interview questions to help you feel confident and ready for whatever comes your way. But we are not stopping there. With this book, we want to outline the methodology, the way of thinking, and the structure for your answers that will make you successful, no matter what question you will be asked, no matter what company you choose. Once you are ready for the tech interview process, you will feel confident enough to prepare for other industry selection processes.

Please keep in mind that engineering interviews are slightly different, and it's something we won't cover in this book. We focus on interviews for Sales, Business Development, Marketing, Project Management, Operations, Account Management, Industry Manager, Client Solutions Manager, Partner Manager, and other sales, strategy, product, leadership, and operations roles.

Before getting into the details of our framework, we will answer some common questions, such as:

Should I work for a big corporation vs. a startup?

What are the career options and the salary ranges offered in these two types of companies?

Do I need an MBA or not?

How can I stand out when applying for the role I want?

We will give you a no-frills view of the pros and cons of corporations and startups and share some of the lessons learned from our own experience to save you time and pain.

Chapter 1

IS IT WORTH IT?
(NAVIGATING THE JOB MARKET LANDSCAPE)

"Risk more than others think is safe.
Dream more than others think is practical."
—Howard Schultz, Starbucks CEO

You don't need to be a founder to have an incredible career. Howard Schultz is an excellent example of this:

- Howard was born in 1953 and graduated from Northern Michigan University. He started his career at Xerox as a sales rep and later became responsible for the coffee machine division at Hammarplast, a Swedish kitchenware manufacturer. One of their customers, Starbucks Coffee Company, was impressed by his skills and offered him a role as director of retail operations.

- After a trip to Milan, Howard was fascinated by the quality of Italian coffee, the number of coffee stores spread around the city, and how they served as meeting points or public squares. He returned to the United States to replicate Italian coffee stores nationwide.

- Schultz's proposal to serve coffee in Starbucks stores was rejected by the owners. Frustrated, he left and started his coffee bar called Il Giornale. A year later, he bought Starbucks for $3.8 million.

- Under Schultz's guidance, the coffeehouse chain grew from fewer than 20 stores to more than 100 in four years. In 1992, he took the company public, and by the end of the decade, Starbucks had some 2,500 locations in about a dozen countries. Today, Starbucks has over 30,000 stores worldwide and over 100 billion dollars in market value.

- When asked the secret of his success, Schultz recounts four principles: "Don't be threatened by people smarter than you. Compromise anything but your core values. Seek to renew yourself even when you are hitting home runs. And everything matters." [4]

Before talking about how to ace an interview or getting into the nitty gritty of interview questions, the first questions you need to answer are:

Is it worth working in the tech sector for a big corporation or a startup?

Wouldn't it be better to work for a consulting firm (in the finance, FMCG, retail, or fashion industries)?

And finally…is this the career that I want?

It depends. It depends on whether or not you have a strong passion for a particular topic, how many hours a day you want to work, if you want to work for a big corporation or a startup, if you like the structured or unstructured work environment, and what type of challenges you want to face. It's hard to make comparisons, but even if it's going through a significant change, the tech sector will still be our society's primary source of innovation for many years. There is no way of denying the world is going (or has already gone) digital. Hence, working in tech means you are central to this change. You are part of the disruption.

---

4 Schultz H., (2024) *Howard Schultz - University of Houston*. Available at: https://uh.edu/hilton-college/About/Hospitality-Industry-Hall-of-Honor/Inductees/Howard-Schultz%20/ (Accessed: 26 April 2024).

Also, in most cases, the salary-to-hours ratio is usually much higher in the tech sector vs. other sectors.

Salary-to-hours Ratio = Average Salary per Hour ÷ Number of Hours worked

On average, you will earn more and have a better work-life balance in the tech sector vs. other sectors because the margins and volumes in tech are usually much higher than in other sectors. Measuring the hours an employee works is challenging, as employees declare that they work more than they do. But for the last ten years, we can say that we rarely worked after 7.30 p.m., and that didn't stop Matteo from becoming a Vice President at Salesforce or Pilar from becoming the Head of Startups for TikTok in Iberia. Ask our consulting, banking, or fashion friends; they can't say the same. And we often made just as much money as they did.

We've made good money even though we never worked for a tech company before it went public. If we had, we would probably be on a beach somewhere right now instead of writing this book (which we love to do, by the way).

☼ An easy way to support our claim is to look at the revenue per employee generated by tech companies vs. consulting firms. Here are the 2021 revenues per employee of some of the biggest tech companies (the numbers are in millions):

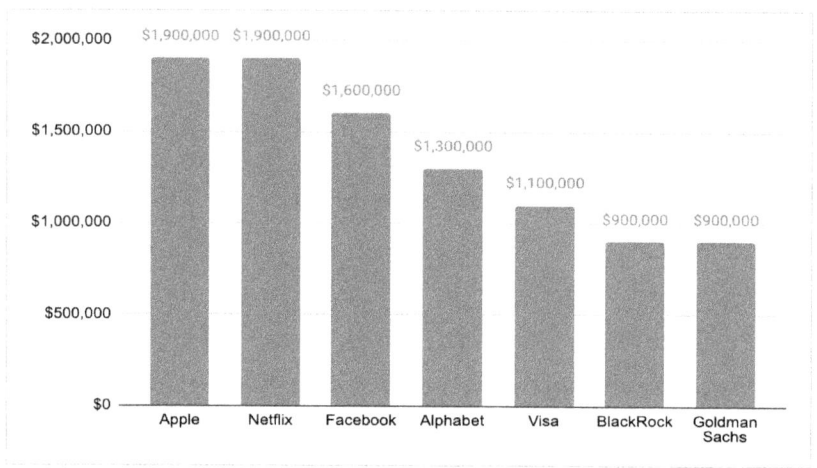

FIGURE 1. Here is a representation of the revenue per employee generated by some of the biggest Tech and S&P500 companies [5].

☼ For top consulting firms, here are the numbers:

McKinsey 2021 revenues = 10.5Bn. Nr of employees = 38k. Revenue per employee = 263k.

BCG 2021 revenues = 11bn. Nr of employees = 25k. Revenue per employee = 440k.

Bain 2021 revenues = 5.8bn. Nr of employees = 15k. Revenue per employee = 386k.

5 Clement, J. (2023) Revenue per employee of leading tech companies 2022, Statista. Available at: https://www.statista.com/statistics/217489/revenue-per-employee-of-selected-tech-companies/ (Accessed: 26 April 2024).

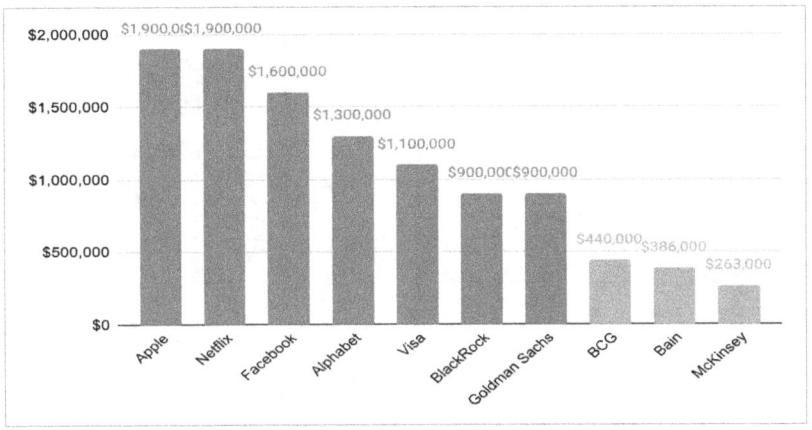

FIGURE 2. Here is a representation of the revenue per employee generated by some of the biggest Tech and S&P500 companies vs the top consulting firm[6].

☼ These revenues determine the salary tech companies can pay vs. consulting firms. They are much higher because of the significantly higher revenues generated per employee. In addition to higher salaries, there are endless career opportunities to grow, shorter promotion cycles, rotation opportunities, and exchange programs.

So, is it worth it? We will let you make your conclusion. Each sector, each company, and each career has pros and cons, and working in tech has a bit of both, of course. But overall, we do believe it's a sector you should consider. However, you should ask yourself another question: do I want this career? Write down your goals and remind yourself who you want to be.

☼ You may have heard of a Yale study in which only 3% of the graduating class had specific written goals for their futures. Twenty years later, they found out

6 Big three (management consultancies) (2024) Wikipedia. Available at: https://en.wikipedia.org/wiki/Big_Three_(management_consultancies) (Accessed: 26 April 2024).

that those 3% were earning an astounding ten times more than the rest of the class that had no clear goals...well actually, this story is a myth as no such study was ever done! However, Dr. Gail Matthews at the Dominican University in California surveyed 267 participants, demonstrating that those who wrote down their goals were 33% more successful. So take a minute and write down what you want to accomplish in your career in the next five and ten years. It will give you a 33% better chance of achieving it!

Life in a tech corporation or startup can be stressful, and there is no point in denying it. Even if you earn more than most other jobs, you will still be asked to deliver challenging goals in very competitive markets and among very competitive teammates. Your day-to-day routine can change depending on the role, seniority, and team; your manager will play a fundamental part. So, we suggest reaching out to people currently working in the company you want to apply to in a role similar to the one you are aiming for and trying **to understand what it is like to work in that team and for that manager.** You will be surprised by how available these people are and by the feedback you might get.

Also, think about the day-to-day routine. What does the job entail? Go beyond the title, the name of the brand, and the fancy offices...**what will you be doing every day?** When you hear "Digital Account Manager at Google," it might not be as fancy of a job as you think! Junior Account Managers spend their day revising Google Search and Display campaigns, trying to devise ways to make their (sometimes more than 500) customers pay $5 to $10 a day more to gain "points" that will make them achieve their quarterly target. It can be interesting at the beginning. But after six to nine months, if you don't like these types of conversations with small customers and don't like running similar performance analyses over and over, you will be dreaming about that bartender job you could have had back at the local restaurant in your hometown!

Also, consider where the company is going and where it is in its development. Big companies are great for stability and perks. On the other hand, if they have a great product and good timing, small companies can offer you incredible growth opportunities. Matteo will forever remember the day he worked at Google in Dublin as Head of New Business for Iberia and met a guy at a bar who had just started working for a new startup called Stripe. He was put in charge of setting up their operations team. He had no similar experience, but since they were a small team and didn't have anyone who knew how to carry out the task, they had assigned him this role. He was talking about the fact that they were in a much tinier and uglier office than Google. Matteo was proud to show him around Google's massive cafeteria, gym, and swimming pool...Fast forward ten years, he is now the Global Head of Operations at Stripe, a company generating more than $20BN in revenues and still privately owned. The day Stripe goes public, he will be a multimillionaire. While we...well, we will still be happy to know that coffee is free at work.

Last but not least, you should ask yourself if this is the career you truly want. The path you take to tech might be a challenging one. Matteo always dreamed of being a filmmaker, and Pilar wanted to be an actress. However, we ended up on tech career paths due to factors such as our education, fear of failure in the arts, and the need to make a living. A path where we are still figuring out what we enjoy doing the most and how to make the most of every job opportunity. We hope you have a genuine passion that motivates your every decision. If you haven't found it yet, don't worry, you're not alone. Based on our experience, working in tech will still allow you to lead a fantastic life while gradually figuring out what you want to do with it.

Chapter 2:

BIG CORPORATIONS OR THRIVING STARTUPS?

(CHOOSING YOUR CAREER PATH)

"If you're offered a seat on a rocket ship,
don't ask what seat! Just get on."
—*Sheryl Sandberg, former META Chief Operating Officer*[7]

Interesting facts about Sheryl Sandberg:

- Sheryl graduated from Harvard University in 1991. After a few brief experiences at the World Bank and McKinsey, she joined the Treasury Department in Washington as Chief of Staff.

- She joined Google in 2001, which was still a startup. She joined as General Manager of the search engine business unit.

- She became Facebook's first COO in 2008, where she focused on developing the advertising strategy for Facebook. Her contribution is considered fundamental to the long-term success of Meta.

- In an interview with CNN, Sheryl shared her secret to success: prioritization: "I strongly believe in ruthless prioritization," said Sheryl. "Sometimes people think of prioritization as only doing things that will positively impact your business, but ruthless prioritization means only focusing on the very best ideas."

---

7 Sahadi, J. (2018, October 3). How Sheryl Sandberg practices "ruthless prioritization" | CNN business. CNN. https://edition.cnn.com/2018/10/03/success/sheryl-sandberg-profile

- Sheryl talked about what they are looking for in interviews: "At Facebook, we are looking for builders. We believe our journey at Facebook is only 1% done, so we want people who can help us build technology, products, and our business into the future. We don't look for a specific background or skill set when we make hiring decisions. As my friend and Instagram COO Marne Levine says, we hire and cross-train athletes."

Is it better to work for a massive corporation, or is it better to work at a startup?

To answer this question, we will share Matteo's experience. This is not representative of all experiences, but we believe it could be helpful to share his story since he has worked for seven years at three different startups worldwide and ten years at two giant tech corporations: Google and Salesforce. He will also share three essential tips to remember whether you are considering working for a startup, scale-up, or big corporation.

Matteo's Experience:

Before getting into Google, my only work experience was with startups. First, I worked for a startup called Atheneum Partners in Berlin as a Business Analyst and a Project Lead. Then, I helped a VC fund develop several startups in Nigeria, and finally, I worked for an internet incubator called Nova Founders based in Kuala Lumpur. At the time, I wasn't interested in working for big corporations. To be completely honest, I despised them. I saw them as these evil, money-making machines that turn every employee into a robot, allowing no freedom of action and forcing their employees into boring, expendable, and repetitive jobs.

So, when a friend referred me for the first time for an Account Manager role at Google Dublin, I didn't prepare for the interviews. I didn't care whether or not I got the job. I interviewed because they offered to fly me to Dublin, with hotels and meals paid for. I thought it would be an excellent learning experience and a good way to see Dublin and Ireland for the first time. As you can imagine, the interview didn't go well, and I didn't get the job. But I started to feel that Google and Googlers were living on a different planet than I was living on. The Google Dublin office in 2012 was massive compared to the 150 sqm Berlin apartment the startup I was working for had rented. All these Googlers seemed quite relaxed. Each interviewer (I had to go through the usual four rounds of interviews, one after the other) sincerely believed that Google's culture and values were of fundamental importance to the company. I returned to my job in Berlin, still proud of working for a startup, but I felt there may be more to Google than I initially thought.

Two years later, when a recruiter from Google reached out for a New Business Sales role, I didn't think twice about it and decided to give it one more try (it helped that the guys at Nova Founders were making me work from 9 a.m. to 2 a.m. every day, for $1500 a month). I prepared, studied hard, and passed all the interviews. And just like that, without realizing it, my life changed for good. I didn't know it yet, but thanks to those interviews, I started earning more than €100,000 a year from that moment on. I met my best friends and wife for life because of those interviews. All while having a lot of fun, growing as a person and professional, and having experiences I would have never imagined.

In 2014, Google Dublin had four office buildings located on Barrow Street — a tiny street not too far from the city center. These buildings offered a wide range of excellent facilities to its employees, such as a gym with kickboxing, yoga, and pilates classes; a 100m swimming pool; multiple gaming rooms with PlayStations, ping pong, and billiards on each floor; a flight simulator; four restaurants; a cafeteria with hand-made pastries; unlimited free snacks, coffee, water, and drinks on every floor; a free dentist studio; four massage rooms with professional masseurs available from 9 a.m. to 6 p.m. with each employee getting several hours of free massage each year; and three doctors available at all times. The office space was so good that many employees, including myself, would spend most of our weekends within the office just playing games or doing sports. Moreover, Google would organize the most exciting parties for Christmas and mid-summer. We would have team offsites at least twice a year in the fanciest places in Europe. With an average age of twenty-four to twenty-seven, it felt like being back at university (but with the added benefit of earning quite a lot of money).

It was an excellent workplace, and life was good.

Looking at my startup experience, it was a rough school of life. It also taught me the skills and fundamentals that made me successful at Google and Salesforce. But damn, I had to sweat for them.

My first work experience was at Atheneum Partner, an expert network based in Berlin. The three founders had worked at BCG, ATK Kearney, and McKinsey and realized these companies often didn't have the information needed to conduct their consulting projects. So, these companies would spend hours looking for experts to talk to to find the insights needed to solve their consulting projects and be worth the contracts. My job was to find those experts.

I would make endless calls daily and send thousands of messages on LinkedIn to any relevant expert I could find to do a one-hour phone consultation. I earned €1,500 a month plus commissions (between €200 to €1,000 a month). It wasn't too bad for Berlin then and for a first working experience, but it wasn't great. Even though I was working hard and doing well, I almost got fired because my newly appointed team lead didn't like me. There were no performance review systems in place, and the HR was composed of only one person who was twenty-two years old and had no experience handling these situations. I had no way to defend my work. Again, there are pros and cons. With the lack of structure typical in startups, you have more freedom of action, and you can have a more significant impact. But if you and your manager don't get along, there aren't many ways for you to turn things around. You are basically at the mercy of your boss. If you are lucky, it's great. If you are not…prepare to suffer.

Moreover, my salary package did not include any stock options or participation in the company. So, looking back at it, the fact that I was working for a startup made no difference. It just translated into having more work and less support/perks/benefits. I did not have more exposure to different topics because the firm was already quite structured and wasn't open to feedback from the bottom.

Tip #1: Ensure your package involves some **equity/phantom stock options**[8] when working for a startup. So that if the company is successful, you can benefit from it and get paid back for all the extra hurdles you faced while working within an "undeveloped" company. If there are no stock options, working at a startup might not give you any particular "benefit" compared to a more developed company. There are just more things that you will have to figure out by yourself.

After Atheneum, I joined a VC called Startup Partners Africa, which was a fantastic professional and personal experience. The VC was formed by two Roland Berger Partners and was trying to develop some businesses in Lagos (Nigeria). On my first day, they told me I needed to relocate there by the end of the week to develop a sunglasses e-commerce business and then a pharmaceutical company. I was thrilled by the idea of living on the continent of Africa and seeing whether or not I could develop a business from scratch. I soon discovered that Nigeria was not like the Africa I had in mind. There were no safaris (because there are no wild animals and there is endemic malaria and dengue),

---

8 Private companies can issue to their employees' stocks in order to ensure they have a vested interest in the long-term success of the company and to make their salary packages more appealing when cash availability is limited. Usually there will be a vesting period for the stocks, meaning that the employee will formally become owner of the stocks only after a certain amount of time working for the company. Keep im mind that these stocks are more difficult to sell than normal stocks because they cannot be traded on normal broker accounts. There are companies like Equity Zen and Forge that allow for these types of trades however usually buyers are willing to buy only shares of companies that have a clear path to IPO (= initial public offering. Basically, to be listed on public stock exchanges like Dow Jones, Nasdaq, etc). Phantom shares are a similar type of compensation for employees as to stock options. The difference between stock options and phantom shares is that: 1) In a phantom stock plan employees do not own shares of the company. This means that on redemption, the plan participant receives cash or cash equivalents based on the increase in the company's stock price over a specified period of time. While in a stock option plan the participant will receive common stocks; 2) The key advantage of a phantom stock plan is that it provides employees with the opportunity to share in the company's success and aligns their interests with those of shareholders, without diluting existing shareholders' ownership in the company. Since phantom stock does not represent actual ownership in the company, there is no issuance of new shares, and therefore no dilution of existing shareholders' equity; 3) Employees with phantom shares might be able to receive dividends if the company releases them to its shareholders before going public.

there were no tours or tourist attractions (because most of the country was in the hands of a terrorist group called Boko Haram), and kidnappings happened too frequently. While most of the expats working for big oil corporations or consulting firms lived in fancy compounds with swimming pools, drivers, and all the services needed to limit leaving the compounds and getting kidnapped, I was living and working in a crappy two-floor building in the suburbs of Lagos. It wasn't fancy. My room just had my bed and a desk, but I had the chance to live the life of the locals and become friends with many Nigerians. I was making €3,500 net a month plus bonuses. Nothing compared with the personal risks I took (malaria, dengue, kidnappers, and terrorist groups), but still, it was a good experience that taught me about living in a developing country, facing a different way of doing business, and learning how to adapt to any situation. Moreover, I am sure that this experience has always given me an edge against the competition.

Tip #2: Go out of your comfort zone and make the most out of your younger years. Relocating to Lagos with a wife and a kid would be almost impossible at my current age. But when you are young and don't have "attachments," traveling and living abroad (perhaps in a developing country) is doable. It will help your CV stand out, and it will help you gain skills and experiences that most of your friends won't have. If you want to enter the top companies in the world, you need to stand out from the crowd. And that can be either because you are brilliant (not my case), incredibly skilled (not my case), or because of the experiences you acquired. Startups often offer these opportunities, so don't limit yourself to searching in the closest markets. Think outside the box and take a chance. You will be in for a wild ride, I promise.

After the experience in Nigeria, I relocated to Kuala Lumpur, Malaysia, to work for Nova Founders, an internet incubator. Developed by two German founders from Goldman Sachs, the company had created multiple e-commerce businesses that were copycats of firms that worked in the US and EMEA, bringing them to East

Asia. I was working on developing a sunglasses e-commerce store across South East Asia. Among other things, I was in charge of sourcing the products and sealing deals with the manufacturers in Italy (several of the top sunglass producers in the world, such as Luxottica, Safilo, and Marcolin, are based in Italy). We would start our work day at 9 a.m., go to lunch from 1 p.m. to 1.45 p.m., work until 9.30 p.m., go for dinner until 10.15 p.m., and then continue working until 2 or 3 a.m. If you dared to leave earlier than that, people would look at you weirdly as if you hadn't worked hard enough. All of this is for 1,500$ a month.

Tip #3: Before accepting a job, understand the company's mood, working hours, and culture. You can ask your hiring manager or contact current or former employees on LinkedIn. This simple check can save you a lot of trouble.

Because of these crazy hours and low pay, you can imagine how I could not say no when Google offered me €36,000 in entry bonus, €45,000 in base salary, €30,000 in variable, and €35,000 a year in stocks. I threw my prejudices out of the window and decided that becoming a corporate guy wasn't that bad after all.[9]

Pilar experience:

My journey has led me through roles in established organizations similar to the startup ecosystem. I've learned that whether or not to work at an established corporation or a startup should be rooted in your values, appetite for risk, and vision for your career.

→ Big Corporations: Stability and Structure

Big corporations are often seen as bastions of stability, and it's true. They offer structured career paths, comprehensive benefits, and a sense of security that can be reassuring. You will find established processes and a global network

---

9 As you will notice, through this book, we have tried to be very open about our salaries. This is simply to help you get a clear idea of what you could expect as you apply to companies like the ones we worked for. We hope this can serve as a guidance and to set your expectations.

of colleagues. Working in larger organizations gave me valuable insights into corporate culture's intricacies and the importance of scalability. I learned the importance of extensive resources and the mentorship of seasoned professionals.

→ *The Thriving Startup Experience: Innovation and Ambiguity*

Conversely, startups are wild, dynamic, rapidly growing, unpredictable, and innovative. You will likely wear different hats, but the growth opportunities could be infinite. Your contributions will often impact you, and you will witness how ideas come to reality in the blink of an eye. I have come to appreciate the adrenaline rush of entrepreneurship, building something from the ground up, uncountable challenges, ownership of your work, and the sacrifices and uncertainties accompanying the startup journey.

One of the most transformative experiences of my early career came at the age of 23 when I embarked on a journey into the unknown. I found myself going to Nigeria, a destination that didn't initially sound appealing. I had no prior knowledge of the country, its culture, or what to expect upon arrival. As weird as it may sound, this adventure was one of my life's best experiences. It was a baptism by fire, pushing me far beyond my comfort zone. In these moments of uncertainty, where I was thrown into a situation where I had no clue what I was doing, in a country I didn't know, a team I had never met, I discovered a valuable lesson. Having a supportive manager, mentor, or guide is fortunate, but life doesn't always provide that luxury. Sometimes, you are left with no choice but to figure everything out. It's a sink-or-swim scenario, and it helps you to become more autonomous, resourceful, and proactive. That's what startups teach. They teach you the importance of adaptability and resilience; you become more creative in overcoming daily challenges.

Another pivotal moment in my career occurred three years ago when I joined TikTok. TikTok was experiencing a meteoric rise then, and the digital landscape was changing. While TikTok's popularity grew, the company's infrastructure and support systems hadn't kept pace. Before TikTok, I had been so comfortable working at Meta. I had the security, the guidance, and the *competitive compensation package. Yet something vital was missing: fulfillment. My chosen role did not align with my strengths and aspirations, leaving me with a pervasive sense of boredom.*

When deciding to leave a company, I follow a simple rule of three: professional growth, personal fulfillment, and financial adequacy. I believe a job should help you develop your skills, surround you with inspiring people, and provide enough income to support your goals.

At my role at Meta, I realized that only one of these key elements was being met. There were limited opportunities for growth, and I didn't feel personally fulfilled even tho I had enough financiall security to pursue my future aspirations.

I've learned that if a job doesn't meet at least two of these three criteria, it's time to consider leaving because you might be stuck. So, I made the difficult decision to seek new opportunities that better align with my professional and personal goals.

Career choices are nuanced and influenced not only by company stage, role, and guidance but also by your life phase. It's not about big corporations or startups; it's about aligning with your values and growth. Your career journey is unique, with moments that test and shape you. No matter where you find yourself, remember that your career should align with your values, aspirations, and needs, providing a sense of fulfillment or money that matches your needs. If it doesn't fulfill any of those, it's time to change.

As we explore the choices between corporate stability and the startup world in the chapters ahead, remember that your career journey is a mosaic of experiences, each contributing to your growth. Let's keep discovering the skills and the mindset needed to get your desired job!

PART 2.

WHAT NOBODY TELLS YOU!

Chapter 3

SHOW ME THE MONEY!
(DECODING SALARIES AND ADVANCEMENT OPPORTUNITIES)

"Believe me, my journey has not been a simple journey of progress. There have been many ups and downs, and the choices I made at each of those times have helped shape what I have achieved.[10]"

—Satya Nadella, Executive Chairman of Microsoft

Here are a few exciting facts about Satya Nadella:

- Satya Nadella is the CEO of Microsoft, taking over from Steve Ballmer in 2014. He grew up in Hyderabad, India, and graduated in electrical engineering from Mangalore University. After moving to the US, he completed his master's degree in computer science from the University of Wisconsin. Nadella started his career at Sun Microsystems and later joined Microsoft in 1992, where he worked on developing Windows NT.

- He rose through the ranks of Microsoft management and served as president of Microsoft's server and tools business from 2011 to 2013, which generated an annual revenue of $19 billion.

---

10 Rani, M. (2023) Satya Nadella Success Story - The Complete Journey of Microsoft's CEO, StartupTalky. Available at: https://startuptalky.com/satya-nadela-ceo-microsoft/ (Accessed: 28 April 2024).

- In 2014, Satya Nadella became Microsoft's CEO. He was only the third person to hold this prestigious role in the company's 40-year history, following Bill Gates and Steve Ballmer. One of Nadella's initial responsibilities was overseeing Microsoft's acquisition of Nokia Corp.'s mobile device business, valued at $7.2 billion. Under his leadership, Microsoft also acquired LinkedIn, the widely recognized business-focused social networking website, in 2016.

- In 2017, Nadella published his book titled "Hit Refresh: The Quest to Rediscover Microsoft's Soul and Imagine a Better Future for Everyone." The book offers insights into his personal journey and Microsoft's transformation[11].

*H*ow much can you earn working for one of the big tech companies? And how difficult is it to have a career in such companies?

It's pretty tricky to share with you salary ranges because there can be a lot of variables. When you get a job at Meta, TikTok, or Amazon, the recruiter and hiring manager will evaluate several factors to define your salary.

These factors include:

- What are your job and responsibilities (e.g., engineers usually get paid more than salespeople, managers get paid more than individual contributors, and salespeople get paid more than business developers)?

- How much are you currently making?

- How many years of experience do you have?

- Which level is the position you have applied for?

- How important is it to fill the role fast?

- What's the total budget available for the team?

---

11 Some mind-bowling unknown facts about Microsoft CEO Satya Nadella. Outlook India. (2024, January 18). https://www.outlookindia.com/international/some-mind-bowling-unknown-facts-about-microsoft-ceo-satya-nadella-news-311805

- How much are your colleagues earning?

- What is the average salary in the country you will be living in? How much more or less is the company paying than the average market salary?

As you can see, many things determine your pay. However, your salary will always be directly correlated with your level within the company. Every big corporation is structured into levels that help distinguish between different levels of seniority and salary ranges!

At Google, interns would start as L2, entry-level roles are L3 to L4, First-Line Managers are between L5 and L6, Second-Line Managers or Directors are between L7 and L8, and Vice President, MDs, and Senior Vice presidents are between L9 and L12. There's an internal rumor that Sundar Punchai, the current CEO of Alphabet, is L18!

At Salesforce, entry-level roles are between L3 and L6, Senior Account Executives are between L6 and L8, First-Line Managers are between L8 and L9, Regional VPs are L10, Area Vice Presidents are L11 and L12, Vice Presidents are L13, Senior Vice Presidents are L14 and L15.

At Meta, interns start as IC1 or IC2, the naming is a little but different and it´s actually called IC instead of Level. Entry-level roles would be IC3 to IC4, first-line managers would be between L5 and L7, (called level once you can be a Team Lead depending on experience and entry level) second-line managers or directors would be between L7 and L8, and after that, there are no IC´S or levels, they start with M1 or M2 depending on your level being managing director, D starts with Director, D1 or D2 (very high) and after that you can become Vice President.

At **TikTok,** entry levels are between G1 and G2, Senior Account Executives are between G4 and G5, while Line Managers are between G6 and G7, then the next step is Director Level.

Usually, **neither the recruiter nor the hiring manager will explicitly share with you at what level you will join the company.** Both at Google and Salesforce, Matteo discovered his level only after his first day at the company, and the same was valid for Pilar. We soon found this was the case for most of our colleagues. Recruiters don't want to share this information to avoid adding another element of negotiation. Moreover, candidates usually have no clue what the difference between the levels is, and it can be difficult to objectively assess your level compared to the rest of your future colleagues. Please do yourself a favor and learn from our mistakes: **always ask what level you will be when joining the company and check if it is aligned with your years of experience!** If you're looking to work at a big company like Google, you must know what level you're being hired for. It could impact your career path and financial growth. For example, getting promoted from an L3 to L4 at Google can take around two and a half to three years and come with a 25%-30% salary increase. Some people jump at the first job offer without knowing what level they'll be at, only to find out later that others with the same experience were hired at a higher level. This can be frustrating. It's important to know where you stand and ensure the recruiter hires you at the right level for your experience.

While it's difficult to give you a salary range, we will share the salaries we were given or some of our colleagues received at Google, YouTube, Salesforce, TickTock, and Meta (in different locations). Hopefully, this will give you a good overview of what you can earn in these companies. Remember, **location plays a significant role.** The highest-paid global locations are usually Dubai, Zurich, Singapore, and Hong Kong. We didn't work in any of these locations, but we have friends who have been working there. To get a reference, multiply the numbers reported below by 2.5x/3x. All these salaries are before taxes, and we show OTE (on-target earnings)[12]. If you are considering a role in the US, you should expect salaries that are 25%-35% higher than the European ones.

FIGURE 3. Here is an overview of the average yearly salary by level for several top tech companies for different roles and locations [13]

	Google (New Business Sales, Dublin, in EUR)	YouTube (Operation/ Trust & Safety, London, in POUNDS)	Salesforce (Account Executive, Spain, Italy & France, EUR)	Meta (CSM, EMEA, EUR)	Amazon (Account Executive, Spain, Italy & France, EUR)
L3	40k/65k OTE 20k/ 30k stocks	45k/60k OTE 25k/30k stocks	70k/100k OTE No stocks	40k/65k OTE 20k/30k stocks	40k/65k OTE 20k/30k stocks
L4	60k/85k OTE 25k/35k stocks	60k/75k OTE 30k/40k stocks	90k/120k OTE No stocks	70k/90k base + 30% to 50% as variable	70k/90k base + 20% variable
L5	(Team Lead) 85k/115k OTE 30k/45 stocks	(Team Lead) 70k/100k OTE 35k/50k stocks	100k/160k OTE Car allowance No stocks	90k/110k base + 30% to 50% as variable	90k/100k base + 20% to 30% variable
L6	115k/145k OTE 40k/60€ stocks	95k/135k OTE 40k/55k stocks	150k/200k OTE Car allowance No stocks	(Team Lead) 150k/ 200k base + 20 to 30% variable	90k/120k base + 20% to 30% variable
L7	130k/ 250k OTE 50k/75k stocks	130k/250k OTE 40k/75k stocks	170k/230k OTE Car allowance No stocks	150k/200k base + 20 to 30% variable	90k/120k + 30 to 40% variable

12 Usually, your pay will be divided between a fixed component and a variable component that will increase or decrease depending on your or the company's performance. The sum of the fixed + variable part is the OTE.

13 Please be advised that the outlined details are intended as a general reference and may be subject to variation based on factors such as geographical location, candidate experience, specific job roles, and the current circumstances of the company. Additionally, it's essential to consider that a portion of the compensation package may comprise commissions, variable components, benefits, and stock options. For example, in 2022 there were 43 Account Executives at Salesforce (hence between L6 & L7) that received more than $1M in commissions.

L8	(Director) 250k/450k OTE 100k/400k stocks	(Director) 200k/400k OTE 100k/400k stocks	(Team Lead) 200k /250k OTE Car allowance 30/40k stocks	180k/250k + 25 to 35% variable	120k/150k + 30 to 40% variable
L9	(VP) 300k/600k OTE 200k/1M stocks	(VP) 300k/ 650k 200k/1.5M stocks	(Regional Director) 220k/280k Car allowance 40/60k stocks	N/A	N/A
L10	500k/2Mk 400k/5M stocks	500k/3Mk 400k/8M£ stocks	(Regional VP) 250k/350k Car allowance 60/150k stocks	N/A	N/A
L11	N/A	N/A	(AVP) 300k/500k Car allowance 120/300k stocks	N/A	N/A

This table gives you a benchmark of how much you could make in these different companies. The numbers reported here **don't consider sign-on bonuses or benefits such as pension plan contributions, health insurance, or well-being perks.** Some companies offer free access to the office gym or at Salesforce; all employees get $100 monthly on well-being (to be spent on things like gym subscriptions, massages, courses, etc.). When considering a new job offer, you shouldn't just think about the money you will make but also about **the network, skills, training, and experiences these companies offer**. To top it all off, consider the almost endless career opportunities that tech companies will provide you.

What about startups?

Every startup or scale-up is a world on its own. It's impossible to tell you what an average salary is per role because it will depend on the financial resources that the startup has. Startups are usually categorized depending on the round of funding they are at.

A **seed startup** has only received seed funding, which is generally the first investment round for a company (according to TechCrunch, the average seed funding in 2023 in the US was $3.6M[14] and in Europe, it was $1.2M). Seed Startups receive enough to start operations and complete an MVP (minimum viable product). Getting into this stage of a startup can be extremely rewarding but also risky because 90% of startups fail[15], and they usually fail because they run out of money.

Standard startups are companies between rounds A and B of funding with a straightforward business model. They are working to develop their products, prove their business model, and gain new customers. They might have received anything between $1M and $50M (the average series B funding is $40M) and are in different stages of development. Joining these types of companies can be a great choice because there is still a lot to be built and plenty of possibilities to grow within the company while enjoying some job stability. If you can get some shadow stock options in your compensation package, you might get a lot of money should the startup succeed and go public.

Then, **scale-ups** are between rounds C, D, and higher and have raised between $50M and $1BN+. These are companies that are scaling up their operations. They have a business model that works, can generate sales, and are now trying to reach the scale necessary to achieve profitability and secure market share. Companies like this are starting to look increasingly like big corporations and can offer great perks and similar benefits to bigger and more established companies.

Whatever the stage of a startup, the opportunity to grow and cover different roles within any of these types of startups is much

---

14 This data and all the other data points reported in the subsequent paragraphs of this chapter were taken from the following report: https://visible.vc/blog/startup-funding-stages/

15 This data was taken from the Bureau of Labor Statistics. "Survival of Private Sector Establishments by Opening Year".

higher than at traditional companies. You will also have many more opportunities to go beyond your role and be exposed to different challenges. For example, Matteo is currently working for a scale-up (Odilo, a Spanish company that received €60M in Series C funding), and he has learned more in the last six months than in his two years at Salesforce. This is because it's a lot more challenging to have such extensive exposure to multiple areas of the business while working for established corporations, where every employee has a role well-defined and structured.

Chapter 4

CAREER OPTIONS
(EXPLORING INFINITE POSSIBILITIES)

"Work takes on new meaning when you feel you are pointed in the right direction. Otherwise, it's just a job, and life is too short for that."
—Tim Cook, Apple CEO since 2011[16]

Here are a few interesting facts about Tim Donald Cook:

- Tim worked at IBM for 12 years, becoming the North American Director of fulfillment and obtaining an MBA at Duke University by attending night classes.

- Tim has been Apple's CEO since 2012 but joined the company in 1998 when it was near bankruptcy: "While Apple did make Macs, the company had been losing sales for years and was commonly considered to be on the verge of extinction. Only a few months before I'd accepted the job at Apple, Michael Dell, the founder, and CEO of Dell Computer, was publicly asked what he would do to fix Apple, and he responded, 'I'd shut it down and give the money back to the shareholders[17]'". Tim's decision

---

16 The quotes contained in this page are taken from a CNBC article: https://cnb. cx/3rmD8xJ

17 Quote taken from Tim Cook's speech to Auburn University's commencement ceremony in 2010, as reported in the following article: https://www.biography.com/business-leaders/tim-cook

to leave a director-level job at Compaq and join an almost dying company like Apple was one of his most challenging decisions. But this decision changed his life for good. His initial mandate was to clean up the atrocious state of Apple's manufacturing, distribution, and supply apparatus.

- Tim Cook confirmed he was gay in 2013. He said he was inspired by Mr. Luther King's words: "Life's most persistent and urgent question is, 'What are you doing for others?'". He realized that people could have taken inspiration from him coming out and decided to take this important step.

- Tim Cook's suggestion on hiring: "At Apple, we look for four key skills: the ability to collaborate, creativity, curiosity, and expertise."

How difficult is it to have a career in these big tech companies? How long does it take to scale the ranks?

The good news is that you don't need to be Einstein to have a great career in any of these big tech companies. The bad news is that:

1. The higher you go, the more political it gets.
2. The bigger the company, the more political it gets.
3. The more challenging the times, the more political it gets.

To be successful, you will need to either consistently achieve your targets (if you are in sales) or you will need to overachieve your objectives and do it in a way that shows autonomy, proactivity, and stakeholder management skills (if you are in operations, project management, or any marketing role). But most importantly, you will need to be able to read the political environment in which you are working: who are your key stakeholders, who need to support your promotion and career advancement (in addition to your direct manager), and who needs to justify and approve the existence of your role.

Every promotion typically takes between one and a half to three years. Once you get into middle management or second-line management, getting promoted becomes a lot more complex and depends on role availability. This means you will be promoted only if a higher-level role is available or if your role has expanded (in terms of responsibilities and impact) so much to justify a promotion. You won't be promoted just because you have been doing the same job for many years. **Tech companies don't necessarily apply the up-or-out logic typical of top consulting firms, but you are expected to keep taking on more responsibilities** as the years pass.

Okay, but what are these career options?

It depends on the roles and types of jobs you choose. For example, for a sales role, the career progression usually goes like this:

Intern

↓

BDA (1 year)

In charge of finding the contacts and phone numbers, ensuring that customers' records are up-to-date, supporting basic admin.

↓

SDA (1 or 2 years)

Manages the inbound leads coming from marketing campaigns and tries to upsell or cross-sell.

↓

BDR (1 to 3 years)

First point of contact with new or existing customers. Qualifies a lead to understand if it's ready to move to the next step in the sales journey. If so, organize a meeting between the customer and the Account Executive to continue the sales conversation.

↓

Account Executive or Account Manager (unlimited years)

AEs find and close new business. Once a new contract has been closed, they pass on the customer to the Account Managers or CSM (Customer Success Managers). AMs/CSMs are responsible for the long-term relationship with the customer, ensuring that a customer keeps on spending.

↓
Team Lead or First-Line Manager (1 to 3 years)
Sets the strategy at a market or industry level and in charge of a team of 6 to 8 people.

↓
Second-Line Manager
Typically responsible for an entire region or complex industries.

↓
Third-Line Manager
Usually Directors or VPs. These are executives with P&L responsibilities.

·

This is the usual career path for someone working in new business sales acquisition, but there are many more possibilities. For example, it's very common for AEs to move into a Customer Success Manager role (responsible for maintaining long-term relationships with customers and upselling them along the way), become BDR managers, or move into Operations or Project Management.

Once inside a corporation, moving jobs and geographic locations will be relatively easy. Google, for example, employs 200,000 employees all over the world. Its internal career website contains thousands of job offers that have not been published externally. If you are willing to relocate, the career options are endless. We had a good friend at Google who changed jobs five times in nine years, living on four continents while staying at the same level and never getting promoted. He realized that even if he wasn't able to progress in terms of levels within Google (changing roles too often doesn't give you the time to get those two to three years of tenure in the role that you need to be promoted), he was still able to leverage the company as a travel agency and to live in many different places, all travel expenses covered! And that's something else you should consider…**more than the salary, more than the perks and benefits, focus on the most important thing a job should give you: satisfaction.**

A great brand on your CV is essential, but it only lasts the first few months of enjoying the benefits offered by a big tech company. If you are stuck doing a job that doesn't suit you or that doesn't bring you some level of joy in your day-to-day, you won't last long. Or worse, you will last long but won't be happy for most days. So, when considering a career option and interviewing, **try to get a sense of what your day-to-day will be, how it is to work for the manager you will be reporting to**, and what the atmosphere in the team is like. **You should consider these crucial elements** regardless of the brand, career options, or salary.

Startups or smaller tech companies won't have internal career sites and might not have structured career paths. Still, employees usually have the chance to cover multiple roles and contribute to different parts of the business, getting the opportunity to try different "careers" and then pick the one they feel more comfortable with.

Chapter 5

TO MBA OR NOT TO MBA?
(EXPERT COMMENTARY
ON ADVANCED EDUCATION)

"An MBA is a great degree for career paths like investment banking, finance, consulting, and large companies. An MBA is not necessarily the right path for starting a tech company. You should be building a prototype, not getting an MBA in that case."

—Guy Kawasaki, Chief Evangelist of Canva

Facts about *Guy Kawasaki*:

- Guy grew up in the challenging Kalihi Valley. His mother was a housewife, and his father held various roles, including fireman, real estate broker, state senator, and government official.

- While pursuing an MBA at UCLA, he worked for the fine jewelry manufacturer Nova Stylings, counting diamonds — a crucial experience that taught him the art of selling.

- Guy's experience with Apple was life-changing. He worked as an Evangelist for the Macintosh for four years, meeting the woman he would later marry. Guy left Apple to create his own Mac database company, ACIUS, which published the popular 4th Dimension product.

- After a few years, he pursued his passion for writing, speaking, and consulting. Guy authored articles for MacUser, Macworld, and Forbes and published 15 books.

- Guy returned to Apple in 1995 to help revive the Macintosh brand. He later co-founded Garage.com, which became a venture capital firm. He has since served as a special advisor to the CEO of Motorola and as Chief Evangelist for Canva.

People often ask us whether or not they should get an MBA. **The truth is that even if you don't have a degree, you might still be able to get a job at Google, Amazon, or other large tech companies.** What matters is that:

a) your CV is attractive enough to get you to the interview stage; and

b) during the interviews, you can show that you will do the job successfully.

How do you do that? By gaining experience.

Start in smaller companies or startups and gain experience doing sales, project management, marketing, or whatever you want to do. Otherwise, try to get your foot in the door through an internship. That will be worth more than three MBAs because that's the only way to learn these crafts.

Are MBAs useless, then? No, they are not.

MBAs can be helpful for many things: helping with a career change, increasing your management knowledge, expanding your network, applying to more senior roles, getting ideas to develop your startup, or getting inspiration for what you want to do next.

Pilar's MBA Experience:

After completing my studies in law and journalism, I embarked on an invigorating journey to New York to chase my childhood dream of becoming an actress. However, my path took an unexpected turn when I was offered a position with a company specializing in developing social-economic reports in emerging countries. This opportunity led me to venture globally, immersing myself in diverse cultures and living in six countries by 2015. During my final location in Barbados, I had much free time, allowing me to reflect. A professional crisis emerged. I had no idea what my other passions could be or where my career should go, and this overwhelming sense of disorientation left me feeling lost about my next move. I talked to friends, family, mentors, and different professionals around the globe, and everyone agreed on one point: take your education further, learn more, and explore other areas. With all this research and advice, I decided to do an MBA, which played a pivotal role in shaping my career trajectory. I would recommend doing an MBA to anyone contemplating a career transition. It will provide you with valuable insights to make important career choices!

Completing an MBA was instrumental in understanding my strengths and weaknesses. Moreover, it played a pivotal role in helping me identify the specific career paths I unequivocally wished to avoid. One of the most significant revelations during my MBA journey was discovering my passion for digital marketing, sales, and entrepreneurship. Through hardcore coursework and practical experiences, I gained insights into these new fields. Last but not least, the networking opportunities that an MBA provides are unparalleled, building connections beyond your peers with esteemed professors and reputable institutions. Did the MBA get me into Google? I doubt it. Would I do it all over again? Yes. No doubt about it.

If you are considering an MBA, the most important question you should ask is **how strong the university's career placement service is.**

Contact the alumni association and check with recently graduated students to see whether or not they received support during their job hunt. After paying anywhere between $50,000 and $200,000, the least you should get is some support to get interviews with top companies. If not, then the investment might not be worth it. Yes, the experience in itself, the friends, the network, the knowledge will be invaluable. But you might be back where you started if the university cannot help you find a job.

What about your grades at university? Are they ***important?***

We never failed a candidate because of low grades. During the many interviews we have been through, we were rarely asked what grades we graduated with. That might be different if you are a recent graduate. Since you won't have much else to talk about, interviewers might be focusing more on your grades to get a sense of how hard a worker you are. Of course, **the higher the grades, the better. You can use them to stand out from the crowd.** But if you were a student with lower grades, focus on the university and the specific degree and avoid calling out your grades and graduation ranking. There is a good chance that your interviewer will not dig into it.

And what if I don't have a degree?

Certain companies will stop you from applying for management roles. Still, the truth is, if you are good at something, have relevant experience, and prepare well for the interviews, there is a good chance of getting away with the fact that you don't have a degree. Don't let anything or anyone stop you from trying to get into the company of your dreams. But don't throw away your opportunities, either. If you fail an interview, in most cases, you will need to wait a couple of years before being reconsidered for a job in that particular company.

Chapter 6

HOW TO STAND OUT FROM THE CROWD
(HOW TO WRITE A UNIQUE CV AND A GREAT COVER LETTER)

"If you want to stand out from the crowd,
give people a reason not to forget you."
—*Richard Branson, CEO & Founder, Virgin Group*

Facts about Richard Branson:

- Richard suffered from dyslexia when he was a kid. He had a hard time in school and had to drop out of high school. Right after he made this decision, at 15 years of age, he started his first business venture: a student newspaper called "Student."

- Unfortunately, the newspaper wasn't very successful. His following ventures were Virgin Mail Order Records, and then he opened his first British discount record store in 1971. In that same year, he was arrested for tax evasion. His parents paid the bail by pledging their homes.

- Two years later, Virgin Records was up and running. It would become one of the most successful music labels in history.

- He is not on the board of directors of any of his companies because he doesn't consider himself a businessman. He believes more experienced people are better suited to run his different businesses.

- Branson holds seven world records. In 1986, he set a world record for crossing the Atlantic with a powerboat. The following year, Richard was on the first team to cross the Atlantic with a hot air balloon. In 2004, he set a record time for crossing the English Channel using an amphibious vehicle.

- He bought an island for $180K that is now worth over $200M, and his net worth is over $4BN.

What if I have applied to many jobs and only received rejections? It must be that my curriculum vitae is not good enough.

These are just a sample of the phrases we hear from our students or friends trying to get a job in a top corporation or startup. However, the truth is:

→ the formatting of your CV (a.k.a. resume) only accounts for 5% of your chances for success;

→ the content of your CV, on the other hand, accounts for 30%;

→ the remaining 65% of your chances of success depend on **how well you tailor your CV** to the job you're applying for and whether you have a **referral from someone within the company**[18];

These are the two things you need to stand out from the crowd and increase your chances of getting an interview!

On average, a recruiter will spend seven seconds reviewing a CV before deciding whether or not to pass the candidate to the next stage[19]. Those seven seconds can change your life, and your CV needs to be ready to pass the test. Moreover, CVs are often pre-filtered by recruitment software, looking for specific keywords to

---

18 These percentages are based on a survey we did to 30 hiring managers at Google, Salesforce, Meta and TikTok collecting their input regarding what they consider to be the most important factors to pass the interview process at their companies.

19 To see the full study from Ladders and get some additional great tips on CV writing, check out this link: https://www.theladders.com/static/images/basicSite/pdfs/TheLadders-EyeTracking-StudyC2.pdf

determine how relevant a CV is for a particular role. So, you might not even get those seven seconds!

So, ***what should your CV look like?*** What is the critical information it should contain, and is there any trick to catch the attention of the recruiter?

- *Which information to include:* name, phone, email address, home address, and your picture[20] should be visible on top of the CV. Then, every CV should include the following key sections:
  - **Summary:** it should be composed of 2 or 3 sentences. The first few words within the summary should match the job title you are applying for as much as possible. These keywords are, in fact, what will be picked up by ATSs (application tracking software) and recruiters. The summary should also give a glimpse into the *THEME* of your CV. What do we mean by theme? Your CV is nothing else but a tool to tell a story: your story. Every story should have a theme, a key message to stick in the audience's mind. In the case of a CV, the theme should be the most critical skill that the recruiter and hiring manager are looking for and that you (hopefully) possess. So ask yourself: what is the critical skill I want to show through my CV? Your summary, job descriptions, and strength section should all emphasize this key theme. One recommendation: do not use empty buzzwords like "experience working in multinational teams" or "great leadership skills" unless you can support these with proof of impact.

---

20 This is true if you are applying for a job in ES, IT and most European countries. If you are applying for a job in the UK and the US you shouldn't add your picture to the CV as recruiters might discard it automatically due to local laws. More info in this interesting article: https://www.jobteaser.com/en/advices/should-i-include-a-picture-in-my-cv

- **Work experiences**: list companies and roles (starting from the most recent), with a precise start date and end date (in the following, consistent format: mm/yyyy), and location.
  - For each company you worked at, provide a one-line summary explaining what the company you worked for did (if the company isn't famous);
  - For each job title you had, write 3 to 5 bullet points featuring your relevant job duties & achievements;
- **Education**: List your education, including any degrees. List your grades if they are good. Skip them if they are not.
- **Your (soft) strengths:** These are things like leadership, teamwork, and excellent communication. It's not enough to list them. You should add one line for every strength to tie it up with an outcome. For example, think of a project where you showcased your selected strength and use it as an example.
- **Your (hard) skills:** These are tools or things you know how to do, like SQL, Adobe Pro, Python, etc. If possible, add the certification entity and date of certification.
- **Languages you speak and at which level.** Again, specify if you have any official certificate that can back up your stated level.
- **Your passions/extracurricular interests: This area is often overlooked but helps make you stand out. A CV should be personal and tell not only about your experiences** but also about your interests. Add a personal touch to your CV by sharing what makes you tick individually.

- *Match the role:* Ensure that **your CV matches the specific role you are applying for.** Any job description will clarify what is expected from the role and what tasks the candidate will have to carry out. Usually, these expectations and functions are listed in order of the priority level. Your CV should clearly show how you can match those top expectations. You should share examples of tasks you carried out similar to the ones reported in the job description. Make sure to use the exact keywords in the job posting to stand out if the recruiter uses software to scan through all the CVs.

For example, if a job post says something like:

Main Responsibilities:
- *Detect and establish new business opportunities in the selected market area.*
- *Retain and grow the existing customer base.*

Then, the description of one of your current or past jobs must say something like:

- I was in charge of detecting *new business opportunities* within my territory. I had a yearly target of $x for new business generation and consistently overachieved my quota, ranking in the top 5% of the regional sales reps.
- Performance was also measured by the *growth generated in the existing customer base* within my assigned territory. I generated an average YoY growth of 40% while working with over 80 existing customers.

We know what you are thinking…*this means I won't be able to send the same CV to all the jobs I want to apply to! Yes, indeed.* And this is because sending the same CV to every job post is the recipe for failure.

Select the few jobs you want and maximize your chances to cut through the crowd to be considered for those jobs. Avoid applying to hundreds of jobs and getting rejected at the

CV review stage because you are not a good match or your CV needs to be aligned with the role. This will only frustrate you and make you lose a lot of time. Moreover, remember that every job will affect your career in one way or another. For example, shifting to fashion or another unrelated industry will become increasingly complex if you start working in the pharmaceutical sector. So, think carefully about which role or company you are applying for. Even if you are desperate to find a job or have no clue what you want to do in life, select a few sectors you might like and enjoy.

- *Focus on your impact:* your CV should not be just a list of tasks you carried out or positions you occupied. **A CV should be a clear testament to your impact,** the results you obtained, and why the company would be mad not to hire you! For example, instead of writing:

> ***Account Executive, from October 2021 to January 2023,***
>
> I was responsible for closing new business deals in the Barcelona area, selling to SMB accounts in the retail industry, and consistently overachieving my target compared to my peers.

You should write:

> ***Account Executive, SMB Retail, top 5% sales performers - Oct. '21 to Jan. '23***
>
> - In my first year, I closed $2M in ACV, with an average deal size of 40k, achieving 115% of my quota and ranking third in my team for overachievement.
> - In my second year, I closed $3M in ACV, with an average deal size of 65k, achieving 140% of my quota and delivering a YoY growth of +50%. I ranked first in my team for overachievement.

The second option stands out. It gives you a clear idea of the results, a benchmark against peers, and a clear upward trajectory. Similarly, when you list your language skills, don't write:

English: Fluent;

Spanish: Basic;

Instead, make it specific and measurable:

English: C1, certified by Toefl on x/y/z with a score of X;

Spanish: B1, certified by X entity, on x/y/x;

Use the skill section to highlight any particular skill that might be relevant for the job or to personalize your curriculum if you have unique skills, such as video editing, public speaking certifications, or yoga teacher certification.

- *CV length:* Ideally, one page. If you are a recent graduate, definitely keep it to one page. Two pages are acceptable if you are a professional with several years of experience. Three pages is too long.

- *CV colors and fonts:* Think of your CV like an ad. It needs to be catchy, easy to read, and visually appealing. Blue and green are usually more attractive colors that our subconscious associates with positivity. *Avoid red and yellow* as much as possible, as they are subconsciously associated with warning signs! Make sure your job titles are bolded, and use short declarative sentences. Use different text formatting options (bold and italics) to draw the recruiter's attention to essential terms and metrics.

Once your CV is ready, it's time to apply for the role. Don't just send the CV through the application form or LinkedIn also:

- **Contact someone within the company and ask them for a referral.** A referral means that someone inside the company (whom HR and the recruiters trust) is saying that your experience could be helpful for the company. Referrals will be prioritized over cold applications, increasing the chances you will be called back for an interview. Don't worry about the fact that you are bothering a stranger!

Most mid to large-size companies have referral bonuses for employees who refer friends and colleagues to a specific job (in Google, employees receive between €2K to €3K, while in Salesforce, €1.5K for every referral). So, current employees might be happy to guide you. It will only take a few minutes, and they might get a nice bonus in exchange for the effort. Just make sure you show that you are passionate about the role being posted and that you are someone serious and worth referring!

- **Find a recruiter within the company on Linkedin and ask them to direct you toward the hiring manager for the position you are interested in.** You could write this simple message: *"Hi! My name is X. I have seen this open role for Z. I would love to be considered, as I believe I have the skills and expertise needed to succeed in this job. Would you be so kind as to direct me to the recruiter or hiring manager in charge of this role so I can contact them? Thanks."* That's it! You might get direct access to the person reviewing the applications for the job of your dreams!

- Send your **COVER LETTER**. A CV talks about the past, while a cover letter talks about your future. It should help the hiring manager understand why you are applying to this specific job, what it brings to your career progression, and why you are a good fit. Very few people write good cover letters, which can make a difference in standing out from the other candidates. Here are a few things to keep in mind when writing a cover letter:
  - ○ It should be one page, no longer.
  - ○ Start with a punch line: *"I'm a strategy consultant with 15 years of experience looking for an opportunity to apply my skills in new ways, and I'd love to bring my expertise and enthusiasm to your growing company"* or *"I saw your job listing, and I was thrilled because it's exactly the type of job I have been looking to apply my skills in the industry X."*

o   Hiring managers will choose the candidate who makes it seem like this is their dream job. So, explain clearly why you want the position: "I'd love to work for your company. Who wouldn't? You're the industry leader."

o   Then you could say, ' *Let me draw your attention to three reasons why I'd be a great addition to your team.*' These reasons should be linked with the theme you chose for your CV!

o   Show that you know what the company does and some of its challenges (why are they hiring for this particular role?). Check their social pages to see what they focus on now, as it can give you ideas on what to write.

o   Explain how you solved a similar problem or task in the past or share a relevant accomplishment. You want to provide evidence of the things that set you apart.

o   You can include a sentence or two about your background and relevant experience but don't rehash your résumé.

o   When you use examples from your experience, you need to give the following:

   ■   Setting: The place where the event of your story occurs.

   ■   Characters: The people involved in and impacted by the inciting incident of your story

   ■   Conflict: The inciting incident that causes you and the other characters in your story to take action. What problem were you trying to solve together?

   ■   The results: What was the outcome? What makes the hero of a story heroic? Saving the day — or resolving some kind of conflict.

- o If you have a personal connection with the company or someone who works there, mention it in the first sentence or two and address the cover letter to the hiring manager (if you know who it is).
- o What NOT to include?
  - *"I'm applying for X job that I saw in Y place"*...it's a waste of time and does not add anything to make you stand out.

We have launched a company that supports students and professionals trying to enter the tech world.

The company is called Gogotechy (gogotechy.com), and we provide the following:

1) **CV reviewing and formatting** to help you stand out from the crowd;

2) **Direct connection with professionals** who are working within the company of your dreams and who are in our network to see if you can obtain a referral;

3) **1:1 coaching to help you prepare for your interviews**, leveraging the tips and methodology in this book and helping you acquire all the fundamental knowledge to pass the so-called "role-related" questions for jobs in the Sales, Marketing, and Operations areas. Plus, we will obtain many more insights by running live mock interviews with you. We will analyze your answers, attitude, and communication style to give you tailored tips and solutions that will exponentially increase the chances of you acing any interview.

It's not always as easy as we would like, but through hard work and with patience, we have already helped dozens of candidates get the job of their dreams in some of the best tech companies in the world.

PART 3.

MAKE IT OR BREAK IT

Chapter 7

MASTERING THE INTERVIEW PROCESS

(SOME INSIDER'S TIPS ON HOW TO ACE AN INTERVIEW)

"Chase the vision, not the money;
the money will end up following you".
—*Tony Hsieh, former Zappos CEO.*

Here are a few exciting highlights from Tony's life, who died in a fire at the young age of 46[21]:

• While studying Computer Sciences at Harvard, Tony tried to launch his first startup (securing the rights to sell pizza to his dorm peers). Even if this first entrepreneurial attempt failed, he could still get funding from the same founder (the mother of one of his classmates) to kick off his second project, LinkExchange, an advertising network. This venture was a notable success, and Microsoft acquired it for $265 million in 1998, only two years from its inception.

• With this money, he founded a Venture Capital fund. And that's when an even younger entrepreneur, Nick Swinmurn, left a voicemail on his phone with the idea to start an online shoe retailer (Shoesite, now called Zappos)—a wild thought at the time to assume customers would buy something unseen that they needed to ensure fit properly and looked good on them.

21 Kang, J.C. (2023) Tony Hsieh and the emptiness of the tech-mogul myth, The New Yorker. Available at: https://www.newyorker.com/news/our-columnists/tony-hsieh-and-the-emptiness-of-the-tech-mogul-myth.

- Tony's idea that customers could return their shoes without questions was at the core of Zappos's success. This proved to be a culture-defining thing, putting the customers at the center of everything Zappos did.

- Amazon, then just about to expand from selling books to selling retail items, approached Tony to acquire Zappos. Four years after the initial conversations, Tony sold the company for $1.2bn in stocks, remaining at the company's helm.

- He tried implementing a groundbreaking management philosophy called "holacracy". In this system, every employee at Zappos had no titles, managers, or hierarchies. Unfortunately, the experiment was not successful, as one out of every seven employees chose to take a buyout[22].

E very big tech company and most startups structure their interviews into three, four, or sometimes even six rounds.

The goal is twofold:

1. Ensure that you are being judged relatively;

2. Minimize the risks of a wrong hire by ensuring multiple people evaluate you across many dimensions.

Your direct manager and most important stakeholders will usually be involved. Hiring the wrong talent can translate into a massive monetary and time loss for these companies, so the interview process is quite thorough to minimize mistakes.

Google, for example, structures its interviews across four areas: logical reasoning skills, role-related knowledge, leadership skills, and Googliness (whether or not you are a good fit with Google's culture and values). On the other hand, Salesforce doesn't

22 Au-Yeung, A. (2020, December 7). Tony Hsieh's American tragedy: The self-destructive last months of the Zappos visionary. Forbes. https://www.forbes.com/sites/angelauyeung/2020/12/04/tony-hsiehs-american-tragedy-the-self-destructive-last-months-of-the-zappos-visionary/

precisely call out the areas of assessment. However, their interview process aims to assess the following: Do you have the intellectual skills to progress within the company and have an impact? Do you have enough experience to do the job? Can you work in a team and be a great asset to the company?

So, while each company might have a slightly different interview structure, they all conduct their interviews to evaluate a candidate across roughly the exact four dimensions Google defined. To do so, they will all organize a series of 1:1 interviews, each forty-five minutes to one hour long. Some companies might use an online test to filter out most candidates; others organize a panel where you will be asked to present a slide deck. All companies will have a first screening call with the recruiter or headhunter, where you will be asked to go through your CV to see if your experiences fit the role they are looking for. The recruiter will ask a few screening questions to see if you have the knowledge required to at least entertain the interviews.

Whatever the process or question, you should know what interviewers are looking for and what they are evaluating you on. Most of this information is in the job posting; you must learn to read between the lines!

INSIDERS' TIPS - Expert nr 1.

Interview with Virginia Manocchio: EMEA Program Manager Google Local Services. 12/12/2023, Barcelona

Question 1: Can you explain what a Program Manager does at Google?

A Program Manager makes things happen, owns an area, and has to keep the right people in communication and orchestrate their work. To do so, the Program Manager needs to know what needs to be done and find a way to make different people, resources, and goals work together to deliver against a specific deliverable. The Program Manager is in charge of scheduling meetings, taking notes, and keeping everything tidy so that other teams understand what has been done and needs to be done. In this role, you must influence and lead critical decision-makers across many teams — the difference between a Project Manager and a Program Manager. A Project Manager is someone focused on a specific project that has to be executed from beginning to end (with more or less guidance depending on seniority) within a fixed end date. Instead, a program manager focuses on the long-term strategy of an entire program.

Question 2: Which skills are fundamental for a successful Program Manager?

It is critical to prioritization to be organized, patient, networked, and ruthless. A Program Manager must understand different roles and their OKRs to push the right levers and ensure everyone contributes to the program's success. A Program Manager doesn't need to know everything happening at a technical level. Still, they need to understand the key milestones, when they need to be executed, and their impact on the business.

Question 3: Which questions do you ask the most during your interviews?

Some of the most common questions I ask are:

1) Tell me about the most successful or impactful complex project you participated in.

2) What was your role?

3) Why was it impactful?

4) What are your key takeaways?

The ideal answer to these questions gives me an idea of the project's context and end goal. The candidate should share a summary of the critical information and data she gathered (main stakeholders, metrics, resources) before starting the project and the key milestones and desired outcomes.

Then, I will want to know how she specifically contributed to the project, what she would have done differently, and why she is proud of the project!

Other interesting questions could be:

5) List the key topics or steps to consider when managing a project or program.

With this question, I want to understand if the candidate has a clear and consistent mental map for tackling a program. The candidate should have clear the need to identify the key deliverables and milestones to be achieved, the expectations of those that assigned the project in the first place, the key stakeholders involved, the metrics we would be tracking if there are other resources needed to complete the project, what can go wrong, and how to mitigate the risks. The candidate should have a timeline in mind, and then, at the end of each project, should aim to complete a post-mortem to analyze everything that went wrong to learn from the mistakes and improve.

6) You have multiple projects simultaneously; how would you prioritize your work?

When there is a question about prioritizing tasks, I always suggest creating a matrix of urgency and importance. Depending on the projects' actual impact on revenue, customers, and time needed, I would first focus on the quick wins and reset the expectations for those projects that require more urgency and importance.

7) How do you find common ground when managing a program with multiple stakeholders and different OKRs and objectives?

It would help if you understood the OKRs of the different teams and how the project you are leading can add value to their teams and OKRs. It would also help if you analyzed the impact on the company and the teams they can use in their day-to-day jobs.

INSIDERS' TIPS - Expert nr . 2
Interview with Francesco Petrosino: Southern Europe BDR Director @Salesforce. 09/01/2024, Milan

Question 1: What are the most critical skills you are looking for in a BDR (Business Development Representative)?

Attitude is critical for me. I will focus all my interviews on understanding how the candidate would face certain situations, and from there, I can infer whether they have the attitude to be a successful BDR. A BDR will receive a lot of noes from customers. So, we look for people who can persevere without losing their positive attitude when things get tough. Also, BDRs almost always support the sales team, so BDRs need to be able to work in a team and handle complex stakeholder relations.

Resourcefulness is another essential skill. When you don't have all the necessary information, you will work hard to find what's missing and fill gaps in your intel.

Essentially, BDRs must be willing to try different approaches and develop new ideas to open a territory or generate leads, never taking no as the final answer. I need to see these skills in the answers, so they must be able to bring up examples that showcase these skills. Accepting failure is fundamental.

Business acumen is also another critical skill. They need to be able to review the data, what worked, what didn't, and where they had success. It will be fundamental to have a structured approach to their pipeline and territory. And finally, coachability. Usually, BDRs are pretty young and in their first professional experience. They need to be willing to listen and eager to learn. If you come here thinking you know it all, you will never succeed and will not be the right fit for Salesforce.

Question 2: What are your typical questions during an interview?

I ask questions to spot the skills mentioned above:

How would you approach a new territory in a structured way?

I want to see if they can develop a strategy that clearly states the final objective, the data they would consider, and the logic they would apply to prioritize actions.

What would you do if you were not able to reach your target? What would you do if you were halfway in the quarter and still at 10% of your target?

This question helps me understand if they have faced high-pressure situations before and whether they could turn things around or devise an improvement plan. It's OK if they did so by asking for help from their managers or colleagues, but I need to hear that they have been proactive and did everything they could to turn things around.

Give me an example of a situation where you turned around a complicated relationship with a stakeholder.

With this example, I would like the candidate to show me that they understand the drivers of different stakeholders and how to align conflicting personalities towards common goals. It's not easy, but by being empathic and having a good EQ, I believe it's always possible.

What new skills did you develop recently and why?

BDRs need to be eager to learn. It can be a professional skill or a new personal skill. The eagerness to learn is something you cannot teach. Something is wrong if people ages twenty to twenty-five tell me they haven't learned anything recently.

Give me an example of the harsh feedback you received. How did you handle it? What did you do about it?

I want to see how they can take feedback, stop and reflect on what happened, and react positively.

Question 3: What makes you choose one candidate over another?

I consider what type of preparation the candidate went through before the interview. Often, BDRs are coming fresh from university. So, they don't have any job experience that makes them stand out. For this reason, I believe it's a key indicator if the candidate prepared well in advance to bring knowledge that others might not have. For example, I would like them to understand what is vital for me as an interviewer, what Salesforce is, how we stand out from the competition, what the most recent news is about our strategy, etc. It's proof that they will work hard to get what they want. Also, I am OK with them not having direct experience doing a BDR job. However, I must see that they own the fundamental soft skills that are key to a successful sales career. I have hired people from very different backgrounds, often with no experience in sales. That never stopped anyone from becoming a great BDR.

Interview with Edu Riera, Head of Measurement Iberia @Meta. Madrid, 19/01/2024

Question nr.1: How do you ensure you are hiring the right person?

I always focus on whether people can think on their feet and logically. Often, I ask: "How many straws can fit in a bottle of 1 liter?". This question doesn't have a right or wrong answer, but it's aimed at seeing what people can come up with and whether they can develop logical reasoning to conclude. I also always try to give preference to candidates referred by someone I know or someone from within the company. It reduces the risks of hiring someone who will then reveal to be something else entirely. It's true that if you do 5 or 6 interviews, the risks of hiring the wrong person are lower, but that's not always possible as it requires a significant time investment from the entire team and the company. So when we can only do 2 or 3 interviews, I rely a lot on referrals.

Question nr.2: What are "red flags" for you during an interview?

I look at the velocity with which a candidate answers a question. It's okay to take time to think it through for a moment. But then, once a candidate starts to answer a question, they must go straight to the point. If they take a lot of time, pause too much, or start to hum, I take it as a sign that they are making things up or don't know where they are heading with their answer. I like it when candidates have a clear point of view or opinion. I don't need to agree with their opinion 100%, but at least they need to take a stand, take a risk, and show me that they can come up with a conclusion of some sort.

Question nr.3: Is there an answer that stood out the most or an extraordinary interview and why?

I wouldn't be able to pinpoint one specific answer. I can tell you that I appreciate sincerity a lot. When I ask a complex question, people may get lost while trying to answer it or don't know how to approach it. I like it when the candidate is honest about it and tries to involve me in coming up with a solution. Also, I greatly appreciate when candidates show me they are not in it just for money. This means that candidates genuinely believe that a job is an investment in themselves since they will be learning something new and gaining experience. Money is something that will come as a consequence.

Interview with Alvaro Dexeus: General Manager Southern Europe @ Pleo, Advisor #Startups, Lecturer. Madrid, 12/12/2023

Question 1: *What three main points make you hire one candidate over another?*

1. Authenticity and Honesty. I prioritize candidates who exhibit authenticity and sincerity. If someone oversells themselves, making claims that seem unattainable or improbable, I scrutinize their responses to assess the integrity of their statements. Should I discover any form of deception, it results in disqualification.

2. Cultural Fit and Relatability. Beyond professional competence, I seek candidates who would seamlessly integrate into our work culture. I envision sharing a casual drink or lunch with the individual outside of work. I want candidates who are both professionally stimulating and possess a genuine, relatable human quality. Interpersonal skills and a willingness to connect with others are crucial in a startup environment. I am not interested in hiring individuals who operate alone.

3. Drive and Adaptability. I value candidates who display a hunger for growth and change. Long tenures in the same role or company can indicate a need for more adaptability. I am more inclined to hire individuals passionate about evolving, adding value, and embracing new challenges. Stagnancy is not conducive to success in a dynamic startup environment.

Chapter 8

THE "NAILED" METHODOLOGY
(THE SECRET FORMULA TO STRUCTURE YOUR ANSWERS SUCCESSFULLY)

"Instead of assuming only one group has all the solutions, scout around for those who have already fixed the challenges or have created something promising ... It's really about using collective genius. We can get ourselves cross-organized and solve a lot more of these problems faster."
—Megan Smith, former Chief Technology Officer
of the United States of America

- Megan Smith's journey into the tech world began with groundbreaking engineering projects, like crafting an award-winning bicycle lock and contributing to the construction of space stations—an impressive start to a dynamic career.

- Her passion for innovation led her to work on cutting-edge multimedia products at Apple Japan and delve into the nascent realm of smartphone technology at General Magic.

- As CEO of PlanetOut, she blazed trails in the early days of the web, fostering partnerships with major players like AOL, Yahoo!, and MSN while advocating for the LGBTQ+ community.

- Smith's ascent continued at Google, where she made waves as a Vice President, spearheading New Business Development and contributing to visionary projects within Google[x].

- Her impact at Google extended beyond business. She led pivotal acquisitions of platforms like Google Earth and Google Maps while driving philanthropic efforts as GM of Google.org.

- In September 2014, President Obama named her the United States Chief Technology Officer, recognizing her as a driving force for innovation and progress.

- Throughout her illustrious career, Megan's alma mater, MIT, has been a cornerstone, where she earned bachelor's and master's degrees in mechanical engineering and left her mark on boards and advisory committees.

- Beyond MIT, she has lent her expertise to organizations like the Malala Fund, which she co-founded, and the Joan Ganz Cooney Center, cementing her legacy as a trailblazer in technology and social impact.

It is pretty challenging to anticipate the questions that might be asked during an interview. In this book, we have compiled a list of the 100 most commonly asked questions, organized by question type, to help you gain an edge and become more familiar with the questions that may be presented to you. However, knowing these questions in advance won't guarantee your success. You need a framework, or better yet, a mental structure to help you understand how to handle, react to, and answer any question the interviewer may ask.

Our goal is to teach you HOW to answer questions, not just WHAT to answer.

We'll share a way of thinking that will allow you to ace any interview. Your focus should be on learning the structure and method to frame your answers in a consistent, replicable fashion so that your responses will always be top-notch, regardless of the question. Once you have internalized this framework, practice will be the final element to guarantee your success. The purpose of practice is to enable you to speak naturally by letting go of rigid structures or frameworks, including ours. That's when you will have reached the level the top tech corporations seek. Before we dive in, turn off your phone and remove any distractions. The following section is key to achieving a six-figure salary in any tech company you desire.

We've developed a methodology called N.A.I.L.E.D., with six essential components. We believe this methodology is the key to acing any interview in the tech industry.

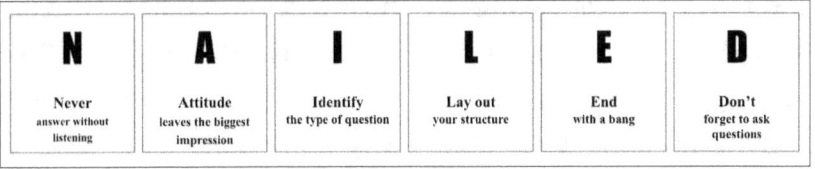

Now, let's explore each step together.

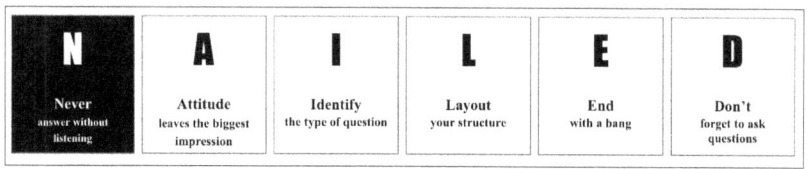

N	**A**	**I**	**L**	**E**	**D**
Never answer without listening	Attitude leaves the biggest impression	Identify the type of question	Layout your structure	End with a bang	Don't forget to ask questions

1) NEVER ANSWER WITHOUT LISTENING

Answering only after listening might seem obvious, but trust us, many candidates don't do this. People are under pressure, so they panic and do not think straight. **Take your time to listen to what the interviewer is asking for and what information is being shared with you.** Listening is fundamental whether you will be working in front of customers or only with internal stakeholders. If you can't listen, it's unlikely you will ever be able to deliver an excellent service to your customers or complete the job successfully. **Listening means asking questions first rather than trying to answer immediately.**

To improve your listening skills, it is helpful to use the critical selling technique called **"mirroring."**

Mirroring[23] is the technique some of the most successful salespeople and negotiators use to establish rapport with their customers and ensure that their discovery calls or pitches flow smoothly without feeling like an interrogation or a series of unlinked selling points. Mirroring involves repeating what the customer (or interviewer) said earlier to introduce a new concept or make a point. As Chriss Voss explains in his book "Never Split the Difference," the FBI considers this one of the most vital tools for negotiating complex hostage situations. FBI agents always try to repeat the last three words the other person has said to create a connection and push the other point to elaborate more on their thoughts. This technique is backed up by a scientific study by psychologist Richard Wiseman. Richard analyzed two groups of waiters.

---

23 Voss, C. (2016). Chapter 2, Be a mirror. In *Never Split The Difference* (pp. 54–56). Penguin Ramdon House.

One focused on positive reinforcement, simply reaffirming what the customer had said with positive words such as "of course", "no problem at all", and "great". The other group focused on using the mirroring technique, simply repeating what the customers had ordered back to them. The results of this study were stunning: the average tip to the waiters who used the mirroring technique was 70% higher than the ones who used positive reinforcement.

In a sales pitch, it might look like:

Customer: I am looking for a car that is big enough to accommodate my family's luggage but not so big that it will be impossible for us to find parking.

Sale: Sure! So you are looking for a mid-size car that is easy to park but has enough space for all your family luggage. Anything else?

Customer: I have two kids. I would also need the interiors to be dark so they don't get dirty too quickly. Hopefully, this won't delay the delivery as we need it urgently.

Sales rep: Oh nice! Two kids…that must be quite a lot of work! OK, getting the interior in dark colors shouldn't be a problem. You mentioned that you need a car that allows you to find parking easily. Will you use the car mainly in the city or for long trips?

Customer: Mainly within the city.

Sales rep: Have you ever thought of an electric car? If you are traveling around the city, that is a great choice for saving money on gasoline. You also mentioned you need it urgently. What's the maximum you can wait? We have a few fantastic options that we would need to order, which could take one month to arrive. Otherwise, we have some great electric models currently used for exposition and would be available today. There are several with black leather interiors, too!

Customer: Yeah, that sounds interesting. I'm looking for something I could take home with me today.

As you can see, the sales rep repeats some critical information the customer shared. This is done to confirm the need and ensure the sales pitch feels natural, flowing like a conversation rather than a series of disconnected questions. The rep mirrors what the customer shared to build rapport, ensure alignment, and link the pitch with the customer's needs.

That's precisely what you will do during the interview. Mirroring will ensure that you listen carefully and get the correct information from the interviewer. As your brain looks for essential information in the interview question, it will ensure that you won't miss any critical information and show the interviewer that you care, are focused, and pay attention to details.

You should apply this mirroring technique from the start of the interview. As soon as the interviewer finishes asking you the question, repeat it to them and ask if there is anything else they might want to hear from you.

Example:

Interviewer: Can you give me an example of when you showed leadership and took the initiative in your past job or personal life?

Candidate: OK, you would like me to share a professional or personal experience when I showed leadership and initiative. Is this correct? Is there anything else you would like to understand or that I should cover?

Interviewer: Yes, I am eager to understand what leadership is for you and why it will be vital for you in this role!

As you can see, repeating the question brings several benefits:

1. It gives you more time to think of a possible answer;
2. It ensures you and the interviewer are aligned on the expectation;
3. It shows you are listening;
4. It helps you spot additional elements that will help your answer stand out from the crowd.

To recap:

Listen carefully;

1. Repeat the question and check if there are other objectives;

2. Keep *S.O.F.T.E.N.* in mind and show a great attitude!

...and at all costs, please avoid saying: "What was your question again?"

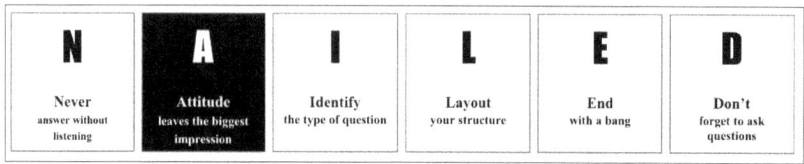

2) ATTITUDE LEAVES THE BIGGEST IMPRESSION

Three construction workers are busy building a wall.

On the part of the wall that has already been built, there is a big clock hanging that says that it's 5:50 pm. The builders are meant to finish their shift at 6:00 pm.

The construction manager, who is there to report on the progress of the construction site, speaks to the first builder. Before starting to chat, he notices that the builder is noticeably low on energy and is working very slowly, carrying bricks from one side of the site to the other unwillingly and clearly with his mind somewhere else. The manager asks the builder: "What are you doing?" and the builder answers: "What does it look like I am doing? I am building a wall. Luckily, I am finally done for the day!". It's 5:52 pm, and the builder drops everything off the group and heads home.

The manager hurries to talk to the second builder, who is working on another section of the wall, as it's now almost the end of their shift. The manager immediately notices that this builder is working slightly faster. The second builder is more precise in his work but still looks at the big clock on the wall every few minutes. The manager asks the second builder, "What are you doing?". The builder says, "I am building the wall of a church." At precisely 6:00 pm, the builder drops everything and heads home.

It's now 6:15 pm, and the manager is about to head home as well but notices that the third builder is still running from one side of the site to the other, carrying bricks, laying out the malt, and putting one brick on top of the other with care, attention, and precision. He is doing all of this with a big smile and is satisfied with his great work. The manager, surprised, gets close to him and asks: "What are you doing?" and the builder says: "I am building the most beautiful cathedral in the world! I am planning to stay here a bit longer just to ensure that this piece of the wall is done so I can start building the next section tomorrow".

Three builders doing precisely the same task.

But with one big difference.

The last one had a clear vision of what he was working for.

To be successful at what you do, you need to be able to see the cathedral. If not, you won't go that extra mile required to leave a mark.

The interviewers and your hiring manager will test you to see if you are the builder stuck doing a task that doesn't mean anything to him/her or if you are the builder who sees the cathedral clearly and is willing to go the extra mile to do your job.

Let's review a transcript of a real-life interview carried out by Matteo while recruiting for his team at Google. Can you tell why the candidate has already compromised her whole interview in the first few sentences?

Matteo: Thank you for coming over! How are you today?

Candidate: Not bad [with a pretty bored tone of voice].

Matteo: Today, we will have 45 minutes together. We will review your CV, and then I will ask you a few follow-up questions to understand your experiences better. We will leave some time at the end for Q&A. Before we start, do you have any questions for me?

Candidate: Nope.

Matteo: OK, you have an interesting CV. You have relevant experiences that could make you an excellent match for this role!

Candidate: Yes, I think so too.

Matteo: Before we review your CV, tell me why you applied for this role and what motivates you to change your job.

Candidate: [Looking down the screen as if reading from her notes.] I applied for this role because I have always wanted to work for Google. I am pretty happy where I am, but…you know, I watch YouTube and use Google Maps daily. You guys are everywhere, and your products are the best. Plus, I have heard you offer some great benefits my current company doesn't provide…

Many candidates **fail their interview in the first five minutes** because they don't show the right attitude or communicate why they are passionate about **the job they applied for!**

At every point during the interview, you should:

1. **Show the best ATTITUDE** possible to portray a professional image of yourself and create a relationship with the interviewer;

2. **Clearly explain why you want THIS job** and not any other job at the company and how this job fits in your career plans. Show them you can see the big picture and how this specific role helps build it!

Attitude: Tech companies are usually proud of hiring people of different backgrounds, ethnicities, and personalities. Having said that, once you join one of these companies, you will immediately notice what everyone has in common. They are energetic, ambitious, and eager to learn. This is not a coincidence. These are the characteristics that interviewers are looking for during interviews. We will explain later how to show that you possess these traits through your answers, but everything starts with having the proper physical and mental attitude.

What is the right attitude? An excellent way to summarize attitude is through this acronym:

S.O.F.T.E.N. = Smile. Open Posture. Familiarity. Touch. Eye Contact. Nod.

Smile: Who wants to work with a grumpy, sad coworker? It's expected to be stressed for an interview, but always remember to smile. From the moment you introduce yourself to the interview's conclusion, smiling creates rapport with your interviewer and shows that you are in control (even when you might not be).

Open Posture: Keep a posture that shows openness to feedback and conversion. Avoid crossing your arms, and don't slump your shoulders (as we are writing this, we can hear our moms yelling at us because we were always eating sideways or bent). According to a scientific study run by behavioral psychologist and UCLA professor Dr. Albert Mehrabian, the person standing before you will like or dislike your communication based on 7% words, 38% tonality and face, and 55% body language (the saw called 7-38-55 Percent Rule[24]). Stand up straight, pull your shoulders back, make eye contact, and smile. You will be unstoppable!

Familiarity: Tech companies are not like banks. They try to avoid the formality and rigidity typical of the banking sector. Embrace this difference. Dress in business casual, and avoid ties and suits.

Touch: Do you have a firm handshake? Do you behave appropriately?

Eye Contact: Can you look your interviewer in the eyes? Are you able to establish a rapport? While you shouldn't be staring, and you should try to blink at least every minute or so in order not to look like a robot, it's essential that you can look your interviewer in the eyes while you talk. This transmits self-confidence and establishes a relationship with the person you are talking to.

---

24 Mehrabian, A., Wiener, M. (1967). Decoding of Inconsistent Communications. Journal of Personality and Social Psychology. 6 (1), 109–114. Mehrabian, A., Ferris, S.R. (1967), Inference of Attitudes from Nonverbal Communication in Two Channels. Journal of Consulting Psychology. 31 (3): 248–252.

Nod: Do you interact regularly and show that you are following? Show that you are genuinely interested in what the interviewer is saying.

Finally, no matter what, be authentic. It's normal to feel nervous, but don't forget to be yourself and chitchat when they give you the opportunity. Remember, it's a learning process. Embrace it and enjoy yourself as much as possible.

And one more tip…**showing your commitment to the job starts with showing your commitment to the interview process and the interviewers.** This means that you should do a brief background check on your interviewer to understand their history, what they did before their current job, and see if there is any passion the interviewer has that you can connect on. Knowing this information can go a long way to establishing a more personal relationship with your interviewer during the interview. For example, you could say, *"I saw that previously you were working at Company X. How has the transition from that company to this one been?"* or *" I saw that you are passionate about football! I used to play on a football team as well."*

It's also good practice to send a LinkedIn connection to your interviewer *before* the interview with a message such as:

"Hi! My name is X. We will meet in a few days as part of my interview process. I just wanted to connect and introduce myself in advance. Please let me know if there is anything in particular you would like me to prepare in advance of our conversation."

Wanting this job: You shouldn't be just attracted to the company. **You should be energetically chasing the specific job you applied for!** The hiring manager doesn't want to hire someone who just wants to work for Google or Amazon. Hiring managers are looking for someone who wants to be part of their team and do that specific role and nothing else. Otherwise, the risk is that, once you join the team, you will leave your hiring manager (who has probably invested hours of their time in training you) for another job within the company. No manager wants that. So, the first thing you should do when asked, "Why did you apply to this job?" or "Why are you interested in working here?" should be to reassure the hiring manager that you:

Understand what the job you applied for entails;

Are the best pick possible for that job;

Don't want to do anything else apart from this job for three to four years because this job is fully aligned with your career goals and ambitions.

Your motivations should be clear and convincing, and your passion for the job should be unquestionable. For example, if you are applying for an account executive role, your motivation should be something like this:

"I love selling, working with multiple customers, and closing deals. I did this in the past, and I believe I am quite good at it, as you can see from my performance stats. This role would further improve my selling skills by exposing me to a new industry and expanding my customer network."

Or

"I believe selling is a key life skill. We do it every day without noticing it. I want to become a master at it, and I believe this job will allow me to do exactly that. Even though I haven't worked in sales before, it's something I have always wanted to challenge myself with, and I believe this is the perfect place to start my sales career. You offer a fantastic onboarding program, your product is solid, and I believe I will receive the support needed to grow quickly and learn even faster."

Whatever your motivation, it needs to come from you. You cannot copy it, and you cannot ask ChatGPT to give you the correct answer. Given your current situation and unique life story, you must find it within yourself to be credible and make sense. If you are still looking for a clear reason or explanation, this job is not really for you.

After you show why you want this job, you can add some cherries to the cake by **sharing essential information you know about the company.** This will show that you did your homework and are interested in the company and what they do. If you have a friend working or has worked there, this is a great time to bring it up, *"A good friend of mine has been working here for X years and has always told me how amazing this workplace is."* This is a very credible and robust rationale that justifies why you are interested in the company.

Other key factors you might want to investigate are:

- How is the company performing regarding revenue, profit, and market share?

- What are the values and mission of the company?

- Were there any recent product launches or releases?

- Was there any recent acquisition or other news you should know about?

- Who is the CEO, and what's the perception around them?

- Who are the main competitors?

- Is the industry growing, and what are the most recent trends?

- What are the essential products/services the company offers, and what are their key selling point vs. other alternatives?

Gathering this type of information can be helpful to show that you are prepared and to stand out from the crowd by showing that you care. You will be surprised to know how many candidates come to the interviews without having any clue about the products sold by the company.

Lastly, watch out for certain **pitfalls that can screw your whole interview**.

Here are the five most common:

1. First and foremost, ***don't be arrogant.*** Even if you are proud of your achievements or think you are the best of the best at your job, never act as if you know it all. You have no idea how many candidates we rejected because they showed no humility. Be humble and eager to learn. Nobody wants a smart-ass on their team!

2. **Don't talk over your interviewer.** If your interviewer interrupts you during a question, follow their lead and adapt the course of your answer accordingly. They interrupt you because they got out of your answer what they were looking for or because you are taking too long to answer the question.

3. **Don't ramble** or talk in circles. Keep your answers brief and to the point. If you are talking for more than five minutes straight, you have already spoken one minute too much. Don't go off on a tangent, either. Always remember the question that was asked and answer that question without getting lost in irrelevant thoughts or ideas.

4. **Don't complain about your former employer or manager.** It's never a good sign, and it shows a lack of respect and confidentiality that will rarely work in your favor. If you want to leave your current company because your manager is an asshole, say: "I haven't found the work environment I was hoping for in my current company, and hence I am looking for a change."

5. **Don't go underdressed.** Just because the tech industry is less rigid, you shouldn't show up in your pyjamas. Consider how you would dress if you had to sell something to a client. You are selling yourself in this interview. Dress appropriately; you can go around in jogging pants once you are hired.

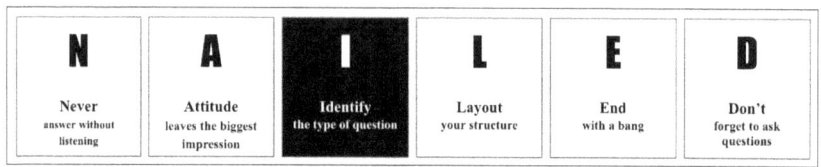

3) IDENTIFY WHAT TYPE OF QUESTION YOU ARE BEING ASKED

Broadly speaking, for any tech interview for jobs in sales, business development, strategy, operations, marketing, project management, trust, and safety, interview questions can be fit into three main categories:

Culture-Fit Questions:

1. **Personal Experience:** Give me an example of when…

2. **Behavioral:** How would you behave in situation X…

Logical Questions:

1. **GCA (General Cognitive Abilities):** How do you solve problem Y?

2. **Consultative:** Should company X buy company Y? Should you open a bar in the center of New York? How many beers are sold every day in Germany?

Role-Related questions:

These are questions specific to the role you are applying for. If you are a recent graduate, it's unlikely you'll be asked these questions as it's a given that you don't have the knowledge and previous work experience needed to answer them. You might be asked, however, a few more theoretical questions to understand if you are familiar with some basic concepts that will be needed to carry out the job successfully (i.e.: How would you generate a high-quality pipeline?, What does CPC (cost-per-click) mean?, etc.). If you have a more experienced profile or are an MBA graduate, you might be expected to be able to answer these questions using relevant examples from your past (i.e.: How did you forecast your quarterly achievement in your last company?). Since the questions differ from one role to the other, we will not cover these questions in this book. However, you will still be able to apply the N.A.I.L.E.D. methodology to address them, and it will help ensure that your answers are structured and to the point.

Having said that, whatever the question, the interviewer is trying to answer two fundamental questions:

1. Do I trust this candidate to do the job?

2. Would I want this candidate on my team?

On top of this, each question will aim to evaluate a particular aspect of your personality, experience, or way of thinking. **You must take ten seconds before answering to reflect on the end goal of each question being asked so that you address it in its fullness and leave no doubts in your interviewer's mind.** Before getting excited and answering the question, ask yourself: *What is the interviewer trying to evaluate here? Why are they asking me this question* <u>*now*</u>*?*

Here is our three-step framework to formulate an answer, depending on the type of question:

	CULTURE FIT	GCA	LOGICAL			
			Consultative			
			ESTimation	Go/No-go	Diagnostic	Brainstorming
Step 1	REAL GOAL	CLARIFY	Elucidate	CONTEXT	WHAT	DEFINE
Step 2	STORY BANK	LAYOUT	Structure	CRITERION	WHY	DISAGGREGATE
Step 3	STAR FRAMEWORK	EXPLAIN	Terminate	MEETING THE CRITERION	HOW	DEVELOP

FIGURE 4. With this table, you can see the three steps you should follow to answer any type of question in a structured and logical fashion.

Before going in-depth on how to answer each type of question, we want to highlight **four key characteristics** that you should always keep in mind when structuring your answers, regardless of whether you are answering a fit question or a logical one. Your answers should always be:

1. **Structured**

   Your interviewer should be able to follow you easily and always understand what you are aiming for. So, you must follow a consistent structure to apply to every question. Don't worry; we will show you how you can answer any question in three steps!

2. **Logical**

   There should be a logical connection between one sentence and the next. The easiest way to do this is to start from the broadest topic or observation and move to the most specific or detailed one. For example, if you were asked to "explain how you would handle an angry customer," start by depicting how you would do it from a theoretical point of view (broad) and then share a specific example from your experience (detailed). Also, ask all your questions before you start your answer, and only once you have all the elements you need to understand the context, begin to share possible solutions. Avoid asking a question, offering an idea, then asking another question, and slightly modifying your previous answer. This would be very confusing for anyone.

3. **To the point**

   Don't take more than five minutes to answer a question unless needed. Summarizing your thoughts is a critical skill. People in these companies don't have the time to hear you rambling for hours on the same concept. Be succinct, get straight to the point, be clear.

4. **Engaging**

   Finally, your answers need to be entertaining. Remember that every answer can be told as a story and that stories stick much more than any other concept. Always refer to your experience, give real-life examples, and describe them as a movie! In the chapter "10 Tips To Pass Any Panel," we will see how panels are conducted at Salesforce and how good storytelling will be central for you to get a job there (and in any other tech company).

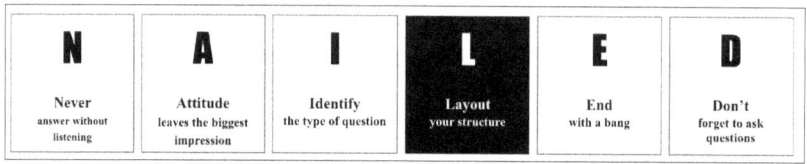

4) LAYOUT YOUR THREE-STEP STRUCTURE

Now that we have covered the basics let's get into the details to understand how to answer each type of question in three steps. We will first tackle Culture-Fit Questions and then the Logical Questions.

CULTURE-FIT

There are two types of culture-fit questions: personal and behavioral.

Personal => These are questions the interviewer asks about situations you experienced yourself. It is expected that you will use an example to back up your answer:

- Can you give an example of when you appeased a customer who was disappointed with a service or product?

- Can you share an example of when you leveraged data to make a decision?

Sometimes, these types of questions come in hidden forms, such as:

- Why do you think you are a good fit for this role and this company?

- What are your strengths and weaknesses?

Even in these cases, where it's not clearly stated that you need to "share an example," you will gain many points if you can anchor your replies to real-life examples of when you showed specific skills. Let's confront two answers to the same question:

Interviewer:

Why do you think you are a good fit for this role and this company?

Answer with no example:

Candidate: I am a good fit because I have the experience and skills you need. I can handle demanding customers, I have experience handling the pressure of a target, and I can work in a team setting.

Now, let's see an answer that uses the example approach:

Candidate: I am a good fit because I have the experience and skills you need. From what I understand, you need someone with experience handling demanding customers. During the last ten years, I have been in customer-facing roles, dealing with disparate types of clients. Last year, I was in charge of the relationship with the most extensive account of my firm, a CPG manufacturer with a high risk of attrition because they weren't convinced of the benefits of our products. They were remarkably price-sensitive and upset with the level of customer support. After many hours of talking with the customer and building a trusting relationship, I understood their pain points and objectives. I turned around the ties, securing the contract renewal worth $5M annually.

As you can see, the second answer is much more impactful as it is easier to understand how and when you show the skills the interviewer is looking for.

Behavioral => *how you would handle a hypothetical situation:*

- *What would you do if you saw one of your closest colleagues doing something against company policy?*
- *Imagine you are now the manager of our sales team; how would you motivate the team, knowing it has been underperforming for the last two quarters?*

Don't be deceived! With these questions, you will also gain many points if you can address them by bringing up an example from your experience that helps showcase how you have approached and will face a particular situation.

We grouped these two types of questions under the same umbrella because we believe they can be answered following the same three-step structure:

- **STEP 1 = Spot the real goal of the question;**
- **STEP 2 = Pick an example from your Story Bank;**
- **STEP 3 = Layout your story following the S.T.A.R. framework.**

Let's go step by step…

=> STEP 1 = Spot the real goal of the question.

Before answering, before picking an example from your past, try to understand the **real goal behind the question**. Try to determine the secondary and primary objectives of the question.

For example, let's imagine you are applying to a Business Development Manager role and, after talking about your past experiences, the interviewer asks you:

Interviewer:

"Tell me of a time when you had to provide difficult feedback either upwards or downwards."

Let's put this question into the context of your interview:

- For this specific role, you know that the hiring manager is looking for someone who will be able to _take on the existing team and turn it around_ since the team has been underperforming for a few quarters in a row;
- _The hiring manager seems to care about the well-being_ of the team and mentioned a couple of times that even if changes must be made, she wants to ensure that the _atmosphere in the team stays positive_ and focused on the yearly target;
- You shared that you have previous people management experience and are results-oriented. Still, _you haven't shared any examples_ of when you demonstrated these skills.

Based on this context, the interviewer is probably looking to gather additional details on several aspects of your personality that might not be evident:

- How do you handle stress?
- Are you proactive when things get tough?
- Can you voice your concerns with the top management if things don't go as planned?
- Can you take responsibility?
- Are you solution-oriented?
- Do you have empathy?
- Can you convey a stern message without being confrontational?

Before answering, it's essential to take 10 seconds to determine which critical skills you should highlight. For instance, you could use an anecdote from your previous work experiences to showcase your ability to be empathetic towards your reportees while still being able to get things done. The more key aspects you can cover through your answer, the better you'll score!

=> STEP 2 = Pick an example from your STORY BANK;

When asked why you are a good fit for a role and company, a simple answer like "I'm great at this job" or "I've done this job before and got great results" is not enough. **You need to prove your capability;** the best way is to present an example showcasing your skills. It can be challenging to think of relevant examples during an interview. Preparing a "story bank" in advance is a good idea. This should include at least five examples of projects, initiatives, or difficult situations you've handled. By doing so, you can use these examples to answer various behavioral or personal experience questions. It's important not to repeat the same story more than once, so preparing at least five (ideally ten) stories is crucial. Here's an example of how a recent grad could create their story bank:

Example	Situation	Task/pain point	Action	Result	Useful for showing
I. **Taking the lead** of my University study group in the macro-economic class	Economic class - my study group was given three weeks to deliver preso re. Libyan conflict and its impact on trade with EU. five team members.	#No clear distinctions of roles within the team. # Didn't do any work for the first 15 days. #We didn't have a clear structure for what we wanted to present.	# Raise the issue to the team # Proposed to vote for a leader to divide tasks #Was voted as leader # Made an agenda defining who, what, and when # Listened to all contributions	#We were able to deliver the presentation on time # Got an A as a result	# **Leadership** # **Execution** # **Inclusiveness** #**Working under stress** #**Team work**
2. **Completing my first marathon**	I had never run more than 5km before I decided to achieve a new milestone and challenge myself to a marathon.	# I never ran longer than 5km # Between Uni and exams, I had to organize my agenda to make space for training	# I came up with a six-month training plan # I changed my diet # I involved my friend in this challenge	# I was able to run my first marathon in under four hours	# **Determination** #**Ambition** # **Going out of comfort zone** # **result oriented**
3. **Internship - helping a colleague** who was struggling	During my first internship in a call center, a friend of mine who started with me was struggling to meet his KPIs	# Each intern had to make 50 calls/week to generate two new appointments # My friend had booked zero appointments in 1 month #The manager told him that he would have been laid off if results hadn't been achieved by the end of month 2	# I asked him if I could help in any way #We reviewed how he was structuring his pipeline and noticed he wasn't applying any particular rationale in his prioritization # I listened to how he was conducting his calls	# I helped him prioritize leads by size and industry # I shared a few tips to qualify the leads better # I supported him, gave him confidence, etc.	# **team player** # **leadership**

FIGURE 5. Here is an example of what a "STORY BANK" could look like.

As you can see, you should write down how to present each case using the S.T.A.R. methodology.

The **S.T.A.R.** method is structured to respond to a behavioral interview question by discussing the situation, task, action, and result.

- **Situation:** Describe the problem you were in or the task you needed to accomplish. You must describe a specific event, not a generalized description of what you have done in the past. Be sure to give enough detail for the interviewer to understand. This situation can be from a previous job, volunteer experience, or a relevant event.

- **Task:** What goal were you working toward? What was the challenge you had to face?

- **Action:** Describe the actions you took to address the situation with an appropriate amount of detail. Keep the focus on YOU. What specific steps did you take, and what was your contribution? Use "I," not "we," when describing actions.

- **Result:** Describe the outcome of your actions, and don't be shy about taking credit for your behavior. What did you accomplish? What did you learn? Make sure your answer contains multiple positive results.

Make sure that you follow all parts of the S.T.A.R. method. Be as specific as possible without rambling. Frequently, interviewees must be prompted to include their results, so incorporate that without being asked. Also, eliminate any examples that do not paint you positively. However, remember that some examples with a negative result (such as "lost the game") can highlight your strengths in the face of adversity.

SAMPLE S.T.A.R. RESPONSE:

Situation (S): Advertising revenue for my college newspaper, The Review, was declining, and many long-term advertisers needed to renew their contracts.

Task (T): My objective was to generate fresh ideas, materials, and incentives that would result in a minimum of 15% increase in advertisers from the previous year.

Action (A): I created a new promotional packet to accompany the rate sheet and compared The Review's circulation benefits with other advertising media in the area. Additionally, I arranged a special training session for the account executives with a School of Business Administration professor who discussed competitive selling strategies.

Result (R): We successfully signed contracts with 15 former advertisers for daily ads and five for special supplements. We also increased the number of new advertisers by 20% compared to last year.

Why is it important to lay out your answer in a structured way?
It will help your interviewer follow your narrative and ensure you can maximize each example. Use the S.T.A.R. framework to confidently highlight your role compared to everyone else's, the final impact, and what you would do differently.

=> STEP 3 = Layout your story following the S.T.A.R. FRAMEWORK;

While having examples ready will help you a lot, none of the examples you had in mind will likely fit perfectly with the question asked. Don't panic!

Pick one of the examples you had prepared, adapt the narrative to cover the primary and secondary goal of the question, and then lay out the example using the S.T.A.R. framework shared above, adjusting it slightly to match the question asked.

In particular, remember the **R** in S.T.A.**R**. = *make sure to recap the* **results** *of your work.* The most common mistake is to go through the actions you took to handle a specific situation, forgetting to quantify the impact of these actions. This is central to showing how you made a difference and why the example you brought up is relevant.

Let's try to put it all together with another example:

"Give me an example of when you helped a struggling coworker."

☐ Repeat the question and identify if there is any other objective to address.

☐ Define the type of question → in this case, it's a personal experience question ("Give me an example…").

☐ Lay out your structure → since it's a personal experience type of question, there are three steps:

  ☐ **Step 1: Spot the actual goal (or secondary) goal.**

    ○ Have I helped my teammates in the past? √ (Primary)

    ○ Am I a team player? (Secondary)

    ○ Are my values aligned with those of the company? (Secondary)

  ● **Step 2: Out of the five anecdotes I prepared, which can be adapted to this question?**

    ○ University project - Libyan conflict study group √

  ● **Step 3: Lay out the example in a structured way -> S.T.A.R. METHOD √**

    ○ **S**ituation -> Description of the context. For example: *"During the Economics class, my study group was given three weeks to deliver a presentation on the Libyan conflict and its impact on trade with the EU. There were five team members.*

    ○ **T**ask -> Adapt it to this question: *"I was in charge of the study group and noticed that one of the team members was never speaking up, was demoralized, and didn't contribute to the discussions."*

    ○ **A**ctions -> *"I sat down for thirty minutes with this student and asked him what was happening and how I could help. He shared that he struggled to follow the conversation because we spoke too fast in English. So, I asked him if sharing this with the rest of the group was OK so the others could be aware and adapt their conversation speed."*

○ **R**esult → Adapt the narrative to cover the questions' primary and secondary objectives: *"Thanks to my action, my colleague started to participate more and more, gaining confidence and sharing unique insights that helped make the final presentation much more interesting and to the point. Thanks to his contribution, we were able to obtain an A. His confidence in speaking English improved considerably, and he could pass the following exams with high grades."*

Note: Check out Chapter 9 - #1 & 2, where we answer personal experience and behavioral questions using the N.A.I.L.E.D. methodology.

	GCA	**b. LOGICAL**			
			Consultative		
		ESTimation	**Go/No-go**	**Diagnostic**	**Brainstorming**
Step 1.	**CLARIFY**	Elucidate	**CONTEXT**	**WHAT**	**DEFINE**
Step 2.	**LAYOUT**	Structure	**CRITERION**	**WHY**	**DISAGGREGATE**
Step 3.	**EXPLAIN**	Terminate	**MEETING THE CRITERION**	**HOW**	**DEVELOP**

Logical questions can be broken down into two subtypes:

- **GCA = General Cognitive Abilities type of questions.** Google[25] defines this type of question: *"Open-ended questions to learn how you approach and solve problems. There's no one right way to answer — your ability to explain your thought process and how you use data to inform decisions is the most important."* These questions

25 Google. (n.d.-b). Google Students Virtual Series EMEA - 2021. Google. https://careersonair.withgoogle.com/events/google-students-virtual-series-emea-2021/watch?talk=gca-workshop

give you a complex problem or task, and see how you would handle the situation through your reasoning skills. You must walk the interviewer through the logic and reasoning you are adopting to solve the questions. Here are some examples of GCA questions (more examples of GCA questions in the appendix):

- *You have been assigned a significant project and are halfway through when you realize you've made a mistake that requires you to go back to the beginning to fix it. How would you handle that while still trying to make your deadline?*

- *Imagine you have been asked to design a customer support operation for self-driving cars before a widespread launch in [country]. Walk me through some of your primary considerations when developing a proposal.*

- **Consulting questions** = Typical of consulting firms but are also used by tech companies to see if you have business acumen and can think about your fit. While there are many types of questions and possible frameworks to use to address them, these questions can be grouped into four major types:

1. *Estimation questions*: How many beers are consumed in one day in Australia?

2. *Go/no-go questions*: IBM wants to enter the video streaming industry. Should it invest in creating a new platform?

3. *Diagnostic questions*: Microsoft has been experiencing a decline in profit for the last two years. What's happening, and how can they solve the issue?

4. *Brainstorming questions*: The Uruguayan government plans to launch a new educational program to reduce illiteracy. How could they determine the success of their program?

We are going to tackle these types of questions in a second. But first, a few tips:

NOTE-TAKING: You must take notes and write down the critical information that you are being given during the interview. Be very structured in your note-taking. We suggest using two separate pieces of paper: one where you will take notes of the critical data and assumptions you make and one where you can do your calculations. Write the question you are asked at the top and, to its right, the operational metric you aim for. On the left, write down the data that you are given from the interviewer, and on the right, the assumptions you have made. In the center, you can lay out your structure.

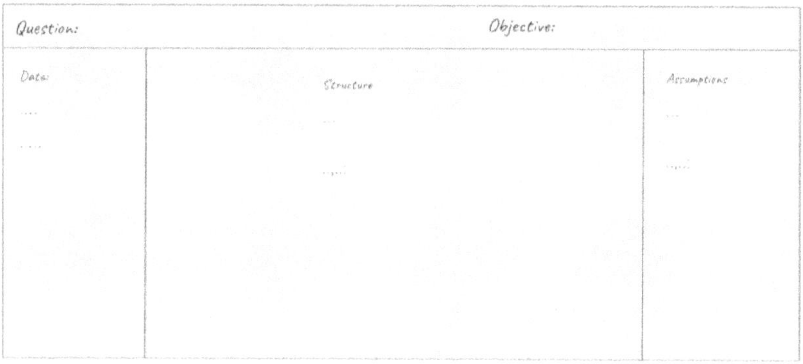

FIGURE 6. Here is how you would organise your note sheet during an interview.

MENTAL MATH: You are only expected to do some calculations quickly by heart. You are not interviewed to be a human calculator. Quite the opposite, if you go too fast in your calculations, you expose yourself to higher chances of making a mistake. **Take your time, and don't hesitate to write numbers down.** Also, **talk out loud when you do your calculations so** your interviewer can follow you. You are expected to know basic percentages and how to handle big numbers (like 1000 × 1000 or 30,000,000,000 ÷ 1000). Have a look at the Appendix "Basic Math You Should Know". We recapped a few essential tricks that could come in handy to boost your mental math skills!

GCA QUESTIONS

Example:

- *If you were tasked with opening a new Google office in China, what factors would you consider before making a decision?*

- *We track our daily targets and our daily revenue closely. Imagine that you notice a massive spike in daily attainment one day. How would you figure out what led to that spike?*

- *Imagine you were tasked with researching your company's competitors. Please walk me through the steps you would take to find and prioritize the information needed for this task.*

Remember that in these questions, "The journey is the answer." This means you won't be evaluated on whether or not the final answer you give is correct. Instead, you will be assessed on the logic you followed. Unfortunately, there is no secret formula to answer these questions, as they vary greatly. There is, however, an approach that you should always use to showcase the logic you are applying, and it's called:

The "**Consultative Approach.**"

Even if these are not typical consulting interview questions, you should act like a consultant trying to solve an issue. And what do consultants do before proposing their solution? **They ask many questions!**

You mustn't just ask questions but also follow **a structure (from general to specific) with a logical connection between them (question A should be linked to question B, etc.).**

If the problem you have been given, for example, is about a business that should enter a new market or that should acquire a new company, we would apply this approach of going from more general to more specific:

First, we would try to gather information about the market by asking questions such as:

- How big is the market we are operating in?
- Is the market growing or shrinking? Ask for the revenue and profit trends of the last three years.
- Who are the leading players, and what's their market share?
- Is there any particular change (innovation, regulatory, merges, etc) that we should be aware of?
- How is the market segmented in terms of customer base?
- What are the barriers to entry to the market (regulatory, political, technological)?

Then we would focus on the company with questions such as:

- How is the business going? Ask for revenue and profit trends in the last three years.
- What's our market share, and how is it changing?
- What's our business model? How do we generate money? What are the revenue streams?
- Has our product mix changed recently?
- Who are our customers? Who is our target audience?
- How are we different from the competition?
- How do we sell our product? Through which channels?
- Are we at capacity, or can we sell more?
- What's our brand positioning in the market vs. our competitors?

Most GCA questions will be more about understanding how you would handle a specific issue rather than a company trying to do something (which is usually the focus of consulting questions). It would help if you learned how to apply this thinking to broader, more generic questions.

Interviewer:

You have been assigned a significant project and are halfway through it when you realize you've made a mistake that requires you to go back to the beginning to fix it. How would you handle that while still trying to make your deadline?

You may accidentally jump into solution mode and throw out many ideas that might or might not work to solve the case. Don't do that! That would be a mistake because it shows that you are not analytical or fact-based. The goal here is to show you can cut through an issue, go to the core, and develop an insightful resolution, starting from the general view to understand the context and then getting more specific to narrow down your answer.

So, to recap how you should handle GCA questions:

=> STEP 1 = Clarify;

First, ask questions in a structured way to better understand:

- The goal/objective and how success will be measured;
- The context of the issue you will be tackling;
- Any other information that might clarify the path to a solution (who is involved and which resources or limitations you should consider).

Candidate: OK, so let me see if I understood the situation correctly. I was working on a big project, and once I was halfway through its completion, I noticed I made a mistake and needed to go back to the start of the project to fix it. How would I fix the issue while ensuring I deliver the project on time? Correct?

Interviewer: Correct!

Candidate: Is there any other objective or factor I should know?

Interviewer: Nope.

As you can see, the candidate ensures an alignment between what the interviewer expects and the problem the candidate is trying to solve.

Candidate: OK, can you give me more context on the project I was working on? What is my goal, and how do we define success?

Interviewer: You are working on a project to lower the false negatives the machine learning system detects when analyzing ad banners. Each ad needs to comply with our company's policies. Our algorithms analyze each ad and determine whether they comply with what is acceptable on our platform. Sometimes, the machine makes a mistake and considers ineligible advertisements that should be able to run on our platform. You are leading the project looking into how to reduce the number of ads our machine learning system suspended erroneously.

Candidate: OK, great. What would success look like for me?

Interviewer: Currently, 5% of all ads the algorithm stops are false negatives. You need to reduce this to 3%.

Candidate: Why 3% and not 0%?

> ☼ When given a precise metric as an end goal, it's always helpful to understand why we are aiming for that specific metric. It can help you uncover additional essential information.

Interviewer: There will always be a margin of error. However, for every percentage point you can reduce, we will gain $100M in revenue each following year.

Candidate: OK, no pressure then... Please tell me more about the mistake that I made.

Interviewer: When looking at the data, you considered only video ads and missed looking at simple banners.

Candidate: I see. I took into consideration only part of the issue. How did I find out about the mistake?

Interviewer: You are working on this analysis with the engineering team in charge of the algorithm. One of the engineers just told you that the false positives on regular banners represent 40% of the totals.

Candidate: OK, a big piece of the pie is missing. Is there any other type of ad that I should consider?

Interview: No.

Candidate: Is there anyone else that should be involved in this project? Who are my stakeholders?

Interviewer: Your manager wants to be updated on the progress, and no one else.

Candidate: When you said I am halfway through the project, what does that mean?

Interviewer: You had one month to complete the analysis and find a solution. The first fifteen days have elapsed.

Candidate: What happens if I don't deliver a solution in time?

Interviewer: As I said, the company is losing millions of dollars in ad revenue every day that passes.

Candidate: During my first fifteen days, did I discover why video ads have so many false negatives?

Interview: Yes, you did.

Candidate: Can you tell me more about the process I followed to find out what was happening?

Interviewer: What do you think? How would you have done it?

Candidate: Can I take thirty seconds to structure my thoughts?

Interviewer: Sure.

[The candidate takes the time to develop a possible approach to this task. After a couple of minutes...]

Candidate: First, I would analyze the false positives: Do they have something in common? Can they be grouped by verticals, industry, geography, or topic? I would do this exercise to find a pattern. If there is one, I would sit down with the engineering team to understand what could be a potential solution. I would do some backward engineering to understand precisely how flagging an ad works and how we can reduce our mistakes in the future.

Interviewer: Good enough. You discovered that 40% of the false positives came from ads in the healthcare sector. Most of the video ads for over-the-counter products were flagged as ineligible. However, these products can be advertised on our platform if they come from a verified business.

Candidate: That's great. Now, could I apply this same methodology to the banner ads?

Interviewer: Probably.

Candidate: <u>What is expected from me to complete the project successfully?</u> Do I need to deliver a presentation on the problem? Do I need to test a few possible solutions and showcase their impact?

Interviewer: You must present your findings and whatever proposal you think would best tackle the issue. The engineering team leader has been instrumental in your analysis and is keen to help you complete this project.

As you can see, **by asking questions, you start to dig out elements and bits of information that can help you get to the reality of the issue**. If you had just started to come up with possible ideas and solutions, you wouldn't have framed the problem correctly, and no matter how brilliant your answer could have been, there would have been a very high chance of failing the question. Moreover, you can see how the questions are logically connected and help the conversation flow naturally.

Always start with the context and the end goal. Once that is clear, try to dig one level deeper. What issue are we facing, how is it impacting our performance, etc.?

Once you have gathered enough information, you can take a minute to organize your thoughts before proceeding to the next step.

☼ Take a minute…you can even take two or three minutes. It's better to take a bit more time and give a great answer rather than take thirty seconds and give a poor answer. Taking your time is also a sign of maturity and self-control.

=> **STEP 2 = LAYOUT your answer.**

When you lay out your answers, go in this order:

1. Recap key intel.

2. State your recommendation.

3. Explain the rationale behind your recommendation.

Let's apply these steps to our example:

Candidate: OK, <u>let me recap</u>. My goal is to find the causes of false positives for video and banner ads and then devise a solution to reduce the overall percentage of false positives from 5% to 3%.

Interviewer: Correct.

Candidate: I am fifteen days into the project and have fifteen days left to complete it. I finished the analysis of the video ad false positives, discovering that 40% of the false positives come from video ads in the healthcare section. Now, I need to deliver a presentation that showcases what is causing false positives in both video and banner ads and develop different proposals to tackle the issues. I can rely on the support of the engineering team's team leader.

Interviewer: It's an excellent recap So what now?

Candidate: <u>My recommendation is</u> to start laying out the structure of the presentation, defining the narrative, the critical information, and the data we want to share. At the same time, we should run the analysis for banner ads as we did for video ads. I would divide and conquer, asking the engineering team to run the analysis while I start working on the presentation.

=> STEP 3 = Explain.

The goal is to make sense of your recommendation, leveraging all the insights and data you have gathered. Don't overcomplicate things. Be creative, develop new ideas, and stick to your main point.

Candidate: The idea is not to eliminate false positives but to identify and address the leading causes. For instance, since one vertical accounted for 40% of false positives in video ads, we could look for a similar trend in banner ads. We don't have to solve all the issues, just the most significant ones. Our main goal is to create a presentation and a workable solution within fifteen days to minimize the impact on our revenue. By dividing the work and working together, we can deliver the project on time. To achieve this, I will request the engineering team perform a similar analysis for video and banner ads. Meanwhile, I will focus on creating the presentation and solutions for my manager.

Is this answer perfect? No.

Could you have answered this question in different ways? Absolutely, yes.

However, is this answer rational, structured, and clear? Yes, it is.

…and that's what the interviewer is looking for.

Note: Check out Chapter 9: #3. We have answered a GCA question in detail using the N.A.I.L.E.D. methodology.

You have probably already seen many websites explaining how to conduct MBB interviews (McKinsey, Bain, and BCG). Most of these websites say there are ten to twenty different frameworks that you should learn by heart. That's not true. There are only four types of questions in a consulting interview, and the four frameworks we will share below answer 99% of the questions. This is even more so when these types of questions come up during interviews at tech companies, where you won't be expected to go into as many details as if you were applying to a top-tier consulting firm. Please remember that the framework you choose will not be the determining factor in passing an interview. It is the thought process supporting your answer that matters. The framework will only assist you in providing a well-structured and logical response.

CONSULTING QUESTIONS

Let's go through the four types of consulting questions, starting from ESTIMATION questions:

Consultative			
ESTimation	**Go/No-go**	**Diagnostic**	**Brainstorming**

Example:

- *How many schools are there in Italy?*
- *How many beers are consumed in a day in Australia?*
- *How much tobacco is consumed in South Africa?*

In these types of questions, the interviewer will be checking the following:

- Whether you can define what you are trying to estimate and why;
- If you can spot the drivers of your estimations;
- If you can quantify these drivers and
- If you can check quickly whether or not your estimations make sense.

Before entering into the details of how to answer estimation questions, there are **three key concepts** that you should be aware of that can help you solve this type of question:

1. Identifying anchor points;
2. Spotting the target group, segmenting it, and focusing on the key drivers;
3. Rounding generously.

1) Let's start by explaining what **Anchor Points** are.

Anchor points are data you come up with that support your estimation and link your estimation to a plausible data point.

There are **three types of anchor points:**

- **Superior:** You know a piece of information bigger than the estimate you are trying to carry out. For example, let's assume you want to calculate how many schools for students aged six to eighteen are in Italy. You might say, for example, that there are 80M people in Europe in this age bracket and that the population of Europe is 350M people, of which 60M are Italians. These are your superior anchor points. These are assumptions bigger than the estimate you are looking for but from which you can infer the final estimation you are looking for.

Based on this data, you can infer the ratio of students to the total population in the EU:

80M (people aged six to eighteen) ÷ 350M (total population) = approx. 22%.

This means that 22% of the EU population falls in the "students" age bracket between six to eighteen years old. From there, you can deduce that:

- if the Italian population = 60M and
- we *assume the ratio of "students to overall population" to be similar in each EU Country,* then
- the Italian student population should equal 22% × 60M = 12M people.

Based on this, you can assume, for example, that the average number of students per school in Italy is 500 students per school. With this information, you can now calculate the total number of schools in Italy:

12M students ÷ 500 students per school = 24K schools.

- **Subordinate:** You know a piece of information smaller than the estimate you are trying to get to. In this case, let's assume you know that there are six schools in your town and that your town has 100K inhabitants. From there, you can do a proportion.

If 100K inhabitants : 6 schools = 60M inhabitants : x schools.

Then:

$$\text{60M} \times \text{6 schools} = \text{360M;}$$
$$\text{360M} \div \text{100K} = \text{3.6K schools in Italy.}$$

We went from a smaller number to a bigger estimation.

- **Comparable:** You know that there are 50K schools in the UK, and the UK has a total population of 67M. If Italy has a total population of 60M, then the number of schools in Italy should be 10% less than the ones in the UK:

$$\text{50K schools -10 \% } \times \text{50K schools} = \text{45K schools.}$$

Anchor points help you set a benchmark, facilitating your estimation process.

☼ Many market sizing cases can be solved using a simple proportion and a minor anchor point. For example, if you are asked to calculate how many gas stations are in London, the quickest way to solve this case would be to say something like: "I am from a town of 20,000 people. My town has 5 gas stations [= minor anchor point]. London's population is 14M people. Hence, assuming that the ratio between people and gas stations is constant regardless of the dimension of a city, in London, there are $\text{20k} : 5 = \text{14M} : x$, which leads to $x = (5 \times \text{14M}) \div \text{20k} = 3,500$ gas stations.

2) Spot the target group, segment it and find the drivers.

Let's take for example this question: "How many cigarettes are smoked in Italy annually?".

> **Spot the target group** → for any estimation case, you need to define the target group that you should focus on to come up with an estimation that makes sense and is as easy as possible to calculate. To do this, in this particular case, for example, you should ask yourself, *Who smokes?* Who will be the subject of this case? The answer is easy: people, and to be more precise individuals who smoke. The only way to solve this question is to understand how many people smoke and how much they smoke.

☼ The majority of market sizing questions can be solved either by counting the number of individuals, the number of households/families, or the number of companies (i.e., How many cars are sold in France? You could calculate this by estimating the number of families in France × the average number of vehicles owned by each family).

> **Segment it** → To define the % of people who smoke in Italy, you must break the Italian population into segments. To identify the right segments, ask yourself: What could be the broadest driver influencing how many individuals smoke? In the majority of estimation cases, it will be _age_. So, let's *segment the Italian population into age groups*. This will make it easy to determine the % of people who smoke for each bracket or age group. Our segments could be 0 - 12, 13 - 20, 21 - 50, 51 - 80. You can assume that the average life expectancy is

80 years and that the population is distributed evenly across each year (in this case, it means dividing 60M ÷ 80 = 750K people for each year). Your segmentation would look something like this:

Age group	Population
0-12	12*750k = 9M
13-20	7*750k = 5.2M
21-50	29*750k = 21.7M
51-80	29*750k = 21.7M

FIGURE 7. Here is an example of segmenting a population by age group.

☼ It could save you some time to know the population of your own country or of the country where your job will be based and the average number of people in each age group, assuming the average life expectancy to be 80 years (for example, in Spain it would be 45M ÷ 80 years = 560Kpeople/year, assuming the population is evenly distributed across the years).

Find the Drivers → For each segment, you can define sub-segments based on the driver that can differentiate between them. In this example, the driver could be the number of cigarettes people smoke in each age group. You could come up with the following subsets: no smokers, low smokers (1 cigarette every per week), medium smokers (1 cigarette a day), high smokers (10 cigarettes a day), and give a % weight to each category depending on the age group.

Age group	Population	No smokers	Low Smokers (1 cigs./ week)	Medium (1 cigs. day)	High Smokers (10 cigs. per day)
0-12	12*750k = 9M	95% of total = 8.5M	4% of total = 360k	0.5% of total = 45k	0.5% of total = 45k
13-20	7*750k = 5.2M	70% = 3.64M	20% = 1.04M	8% = 0.41M	2% = 0.104M
21-50	29*750k = approx. 22.5M	60% = 13.5M	20% = 4.5M	10% = 2.25M	10% = 2.25M
51-80	29*750k = approx. 22.5M	50% = 11.2M	20% = 4.5M	15% = 3.35M	15% = 3.37M

FIGURE 8. Here is an example of sub-segmenting a population based on key drivers.

Subsetting the Italian population into age groups and then into low, medium, and high smokers allows you to develop a detailed analysis. From here, it will be easy to solve this case: you simply need to multiply the number of people in each category by the average number of cigarettes smoked per week by the number of weeks in a year!

1) **Round generously:** As you can see from the table above, the calculations don't need to be perfect. In the case of 29 × 750k, you can calculate 30 × 750k, which is a much easier mental calculation. Let the interviewer know you are rounding up the math to make it faster.

Now that you know these tricks, here are the three steps you should follow to structure these estimation cases: **E**lucidate, **S**tructure, **T**erminate (as for the beginning of the word **EST**imation).

		Consultative		
	ESTimation	Go/No-go	Diagnostic	Brainstorming
Step 1.	**Elucidate**	CONTEXT	WHAT	DEFINE
Step 2.	**Structure**	CRITERION	WHY	DISAGGREGATE
Step 3.	**Terminate**	MEETING THE CRITERION	HOW	DEVELOP

=> **Step 1 = Elucidate.**

Let's assume the question is: *How many cars are produced in France?*
Here, the term "produced" is not precise. You should ask your interviewer to clarify what we want to determine precisely: Are we interested in the cars that are assembled and then sold in France, or are we interested in the vehicles that are entirely produced, from start to finish, in French territory? There is a big difference between these two scenarios! Moreover, what is the time frame that we are interested in? Is the interviewer interested just in the number of units or in their value as well?

Another example: How much tobacco is consumed in South Africa? You should ask your interviewer to clarify if we are interested only in the tobacco consumed by individuals or if there is there any other way in which tobacco is consumed that we should be aware of (e.g., pharmaceutical companies or food companies)?

=> Step 2 = Structure.

Once you know what to estimate, you need to develop a structure. To structure your case, you can use a tree diagram or a table, depending on the easier.

Consider the following question: *How many cars are sold in France in a year?* Anchor points:

- 70M people are living in France.
- Who is the target group? Meaning, who buys cars? You could either focus on individuals who are old enough to have a driving license, or you could focus on "households." Let's solve this case using "households" as our target group to make it more interesting. This means we will try to calculate how many households there are in France and the average number of cars they buy yearly. We will assume that every family is composed, on average, of four family members.
- The key driver to help distinguish between households and the amount of cars they buy could be average income (low, medium, high) and as well the fact that a household will use the same car for five years and then buy a new one.

Example of a Tree Structure:

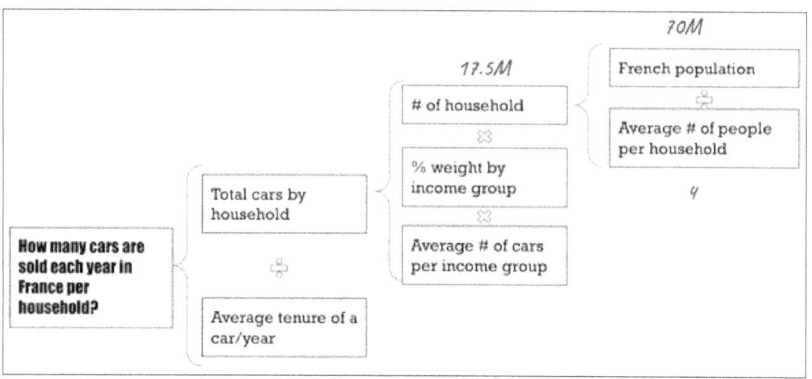

FIGURE 9. Here is a simple tree structure that you can draw to help visualize your case reasoning.

To solve the case, you will first calculate the number of households in France:

**70M people ÷ 4 people/family = 17.5M households
(= Target Group)**

Then, you will *segment* the number of households into income groups, making assumptions about a) their percentage weight on the total population and b) the average number of cars per household.

	% weight	Household	Average # of cars per household	# of cars
Low income	40%	40% * 17.5M = 7M	0.8	7M*0.8 = 5.6M
Medium income	50%	50%*17.5M= 8.75M	1.2	8.75M*1.2=10.5M
High income	10%	10%*17.5M = 1.75M	1.8	1.75M * 1.8 = 1.4M

FIGURE 10. Population in France is segmented by two key drivers: households and the number of cars per household.

Total number of cars in France = 5.6M + 10.5M + 1.4M = 17.5M.

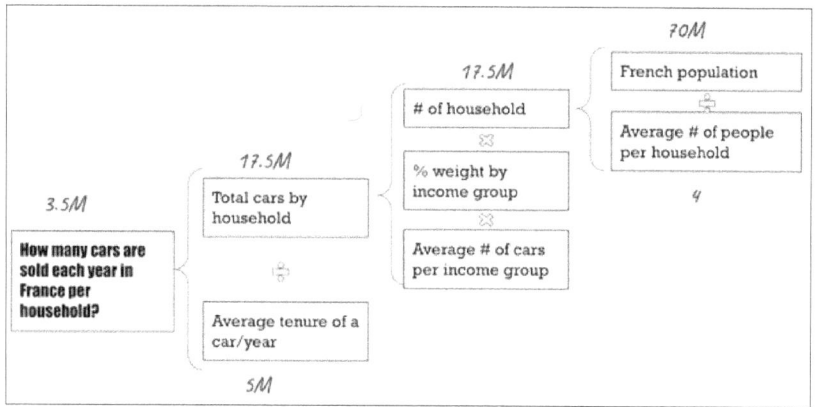

FIGURE 11. Keep track of the results once you complete each step of the tree structure.

Assuming that a car lasts five years on average, 17.5M ÷ 5 years = 3.5M cars must be changed yearly. Hence, it's fair to assume that in France, 3.5M cars are sold yearly to meet all households' needs and demands. We should probably add more cars sold for taxis, corporations, rental cars, and other uses not related to household' use. You could assume that these types of cars equal 20% of the overall car market, so that would be 20% × 3.5M = approx. 0.7M more cars. The total number of cars produced in France could be 3.5M + 0.7M = 4.2M cars/year in total.

You can gain extra points by calling out a big assumption that we are making: the market is not growing or decreasing over time, and hence, we are assuming the demand for cars is constant.

=> Step 3 = Terminate.

Once you have your estimate, don't just share your number.

Double-check your estimate. Try to verify that the number you came up with makes sense. If, in the example above, the final number you got in terms of the number of cars in France was in the thousands, you should take it as a sign that you probably made a mistake in either your math or your assumptions. Use anchor points to verify whether or not your estimate makes sense.

<u>Highlight your assumptions and how impactful they are</u> on the overall estimation. Note the weak spots (the variables that, if changed by a small amount, could significantly affect your estimate). In our first example, we assumed a school's average size was 500 students. If it were 1,000 students, our estimate would be halved. In the car example, we made a big assumption on the distribution of families by income, the average number of members of each family, and the average number of cars per family. Show that you are aware of these assumptions to show that you control your analysis.

<u>Provide insights and implications.</u> Once you develop a number, try to provide insights around it. Is it a significant number? A low number? What does it mean for the industry and the estimation? What should be the next step?

In the example of the car, you could say something like this:

"Since the French population is getting poorer and older over time, there will be a change in the coming years in how the households are split by income, with more families entering the low and medium brackets and fewer people staying in the high bracket. This will further reduce the number of cars sold in France in the coming years."

Consultative			
ESTimation	**Go/No-go**	**Diagnostic**	**Brainstorming**

Example:

- *Should company X buy company Y.*
- *Should company X launch product Z.*
- *Should the government of Zimbabwe close a trade deal with China?*

Here are the three steps you should follow to tackle these questions:

	ESTimation	Go/No-go	Diagnostic	Brainstorming
Step 1.	Elucidate	**CONTEXT**	WHAT	DEFINE
Step 2.	Structure	**CRITERION**	WHY	DISAGGREGATE
Step 3.	Terminate	**MEETING THE CRITERION**	HOW	DEVELOP

Let's go through a real-life interview and see these three steps in detail:

Interviewer:

A friend of yours is considering whether or not to open a Thai restaurant in the Milan city center. He needs your help to evaluate whether or not he should do it.

You can solve these types of cases in three steps:

=> Step 1: Gather all the info needed to understand the CONTEXT of the case;

=> Step 2: Move on to defining the CRITERION, meaning the condition that, if met, would justify a GO decision;

=> Step 3: Understand if the CRITERION can be met, meaning it's doable to do what needs to be done to achieve the condition required for a GO decision;

Let's start from step 1:

=> Step 1: Define the core question & get the CONTEXT.

First, you must understand the question's objective and ensure it is linked to an operational metric.

What do we mean by *operational metric*? You need to translate the goal into a metric you can measure (if not stated otherwise, a company's end goal is always to increase its bottom line, which means profits!).

In this example, the question that you should answer (and repeat back) is:

Candidate: Let me repeat the question to ensure I got it right. My friend is considering opening a Thai restaurant in the Milan city center and would like to understand whether it makes business sense, meaning whether he could make a profit within his desired timeline [= OUR OPERATIONAL METRIC]. Is this correct? Is there any other objective we should consider?

Interviewer: Correct. There are no other objectives.

Candidate: Can you tell me more about the restaurant my friend has in mind? What would be the business model?

Interviewer: The restaurant will be in a central area of the city center of Milan. He plans to keep the restaurant open only for lunch and dinner, five days a week, selling both online and offline. The staff will include a chief, one maître d', and three waiters.

Candidate: What is our positioning in the market? Does he want to be a cheap option or a premium one?

Interviewer: Premium.

Candidate: How big will it be?

Interviewer: 200 square meters.

….

=> Step 2:   Identify the CRITERION to answer this question.

What's the condition(s) that would justify a GO? What needs to be true for opening the restaurant to make sense?

In the example above (and in the majority of Go/No-Go questions), the key criteria are:

a) Does it make **FINANCIAL SENSE** to open the restaurant?

b) Do we have the **CAPABILITIES** (capital and skill) to carry out this operation?

c) Are the **RISKS** manageable?

If both A, B and C are met, we can answer the Go/No-Go question positively.

You could lay out this structure this way:

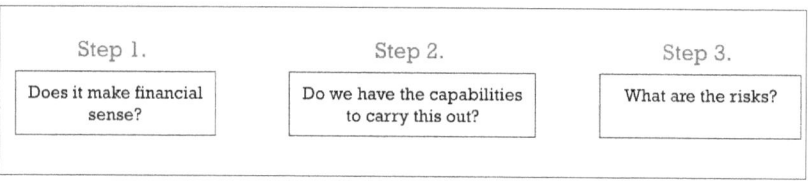

FIGURE 12. Here are the three steps to tackle a Go/No-go case.

Once you have laid out these three conditions, you should tell your interviewer that you will prioritize the first question: does it make financial sense? If it doesn't, the other two questions will not matter. Hence, you won't even analyze them.

For this project to make financial sense, the profit generated by the restaurant should exceed the investment needed to start the restaurant within the timeframe set by your friend. The restaurant could take twenty years to break even, but few people will be willing to work this long without seeing a profit! Hence, it's essential to consider the time frame within which your friend wants to break even.

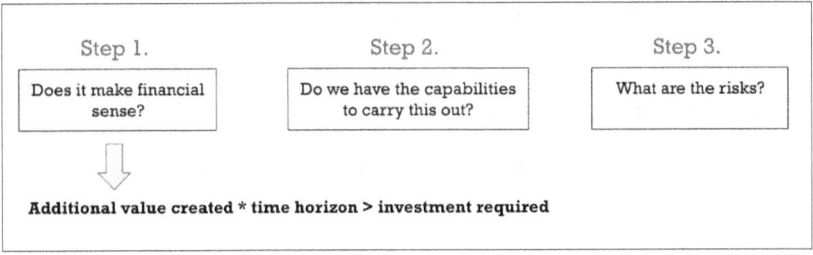

Step 1.	Step 2.	Step 3.
Does it make financial sense?	Do we have the capabilities to carry this out?	What are the risks?

Additional value created * time horizon > investment required

The interviewer will usually provide the two variables: time horizon and investment required. Therefore, once you clearly understand the operational metric, you must address (profits), ask the interviewer about the customer's investment time horizon and forecasted investment.

Candidate: To help my friend with this decision, I will consider three key questions: Does it make financial sense? Do we have the skills and capabilities to execute successfully? And what are the risks associated with this decision? Out of these three questions, I will prioritize the first one as evaluating the other two is essential. Before entering the details, I think understanding " why " is always important." Is there any reason we want to open this restaurant apart from generating profits?

Interviewer: Your friend wants to be a business owner. It's his life mission to become an entrepreneur.

Candidate: I'll keep that in mind. Let's start evaluating whether this move makes financial sense. To do so, I must understand if the restaurant's profits will be higher than the investment required to start it within my friend's target timeframe. Do we know the investment and the time frame my friend has in mind?

Interview: Your friend wants to recover his investment in three years, and he plans to invest 500K to start the restaurant.

=> Step 3: Can we MEET THE CRITERION?

Following our example, what you need to figure out now is:

a) whether or not the restaurant will be able to generate more than 500k in profits within three years;

b) If yes, then you should check if we have the skills and financial means to do it;

c) Once you have ensured you have the capabilities, you need to evaluate the potential risks and whether or not they are bearable for the client.

All the conditions to be met is the criterion required for the project to be a GO.

Let's start to assess the first condition and determine **how profits are generated.**

Profits are simply what's left of the revenues once all costs are subtracted.

$$\text{Profift} = \text{Revenue} - \text{Costs.}$$

Hence, you could lay out the following structure.

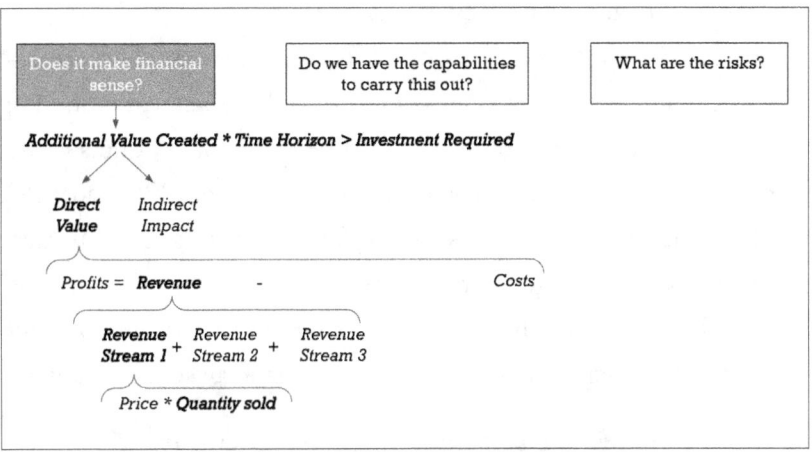

FIGURE 13. Here is how a full breakdown of the variables on the revenue side of the equation could look like.

☼ Before diving deep into profits, we should distinguish between two value creation types.

a) **Direct value** is the profits that will be generated by the restaurant;

b) **Indirect value/impact** represents the impact that opening a restaurant could have, for example, on other activities owned by your friend. This can be positive if there are synergies (like lower cost of raw materials, same audience, branding). But it could also have a negative impact. For example, opening this restaurant will take away time and resources from other businesses. We must consider this to assess whether opening a restaurant fully makes financial sense. (FYI: usually, the fact that you bring this up is more than enough for the interviewer, and you won't be asked to go into detail to calculate the indirect value impact of a decision.)

Always start by analyzing **Revenues.**

There could be multiple streams of revenue that you should take into account. When analyzing revenues, ALWAYS start by defining the different revenue streams. It could be different products or the same product to different customer segments (i.e., B2B and B2C) or different lines of business in different markets. In this case, the restaurant could generate revenue from the customers served at the tables, from selling online, and catering to corporations and weddings. For each revenue stream, you must analyse the following:

Revenue stream = Price × Quantity.

This means that the PRICE at which you sell your goods/services, multiplied by the QUANTITY (the number of products sold), gives you the overall revenue generated by those goods/services. The interviewer will usually give you the price. Otherwise, you can determine the price by looking at the price of your competitors and how you want to position your products in the markets (i.e., luxury, middle, and low price points)).

> ☼ To impress your interviewer, mention the price elasticity of your product. Price elasticity is whether or not the demand for your product changes disproportionally vs. a price change. Let's imagine that you are selling toilet paper. If you charge +10% for a package of toilet paper, the demand for this product may decrease by much more than 10% because toilet paper is highly price-sensitive (i.e., elastic). If you sell luxury watches, increasing your price by +10% might translate into less than a 10% decrease in demand. This is because luxury watches are less sensitive (inelastic) to a change in price.

To calculate the **QUANTITY** of products sold, you should consider the following:

Quantity = no. of customers × average no. of items bought × frequency

Applying this to our restaurant example, you must calculate how many customers you can have in a specific timeframe, how many meals they will buy, and with what frequency.

Now that you have laid out this structure, you need to ask questions to gather the value of the variables. Remember to refer to the structure above so you don't lose your logical flow. It should always be clear why you are asking a specific question to avoid giving the feeling that you are just trying to stumble onto the right piece of intel. So stick to your structure!

Candidate: As we know, a restaurant's profits depend on two components: the total revenues minus the total costs. Total revenues will be the sum of the restaurant's different revenue streams. Based on our information, they plan offline and online sales. For each of these streams, we will need to figure out the average price, which, in this case, is the average bill paid by each customer and the number of meals sold. To forecast the average bill, we will need to consider several factors, such as our competition's pricing, our market positioning, the average price of the items, and the price elasticity of the demand. The number of meals sold via the offline channel will depend on the average number of customers per turn, the number of turns per day, and the number of days it is open in a year. The number of customers per turn can be estimated by the restaurant capacity times the average occupancy rate.

As you can see, the candidate walks the interviewer through the structure to explain its different components.

Candidate: So, let's start with pricing. Does my friend have any data or information to help us determine our restaurant's average bill?

Interviewer: Yes, your friend wants to create a premium restaurant. He expects the average bill to be around €40 per person for offline and online sales.

Candidate: Perfect. Let's examine the number of meals sold. Do we know the restaurant's maximum capacity?

As we don't have any data, we need to see what the interviewer will share with us — starting from the bottom of our tree and going up.

Interviewer: We know that the restaurant will be 200 square meters and that your friend has seen a one-meter-long and wide table he likes that could be used for the customers' tables. Each of these tables can seat up to four persons.

Candidate: This can help estimate the restaurant's capacity. Let's assume that the restaurant comprises three areas: the kitchen, the bathrooms, and the main area where the tables will be.

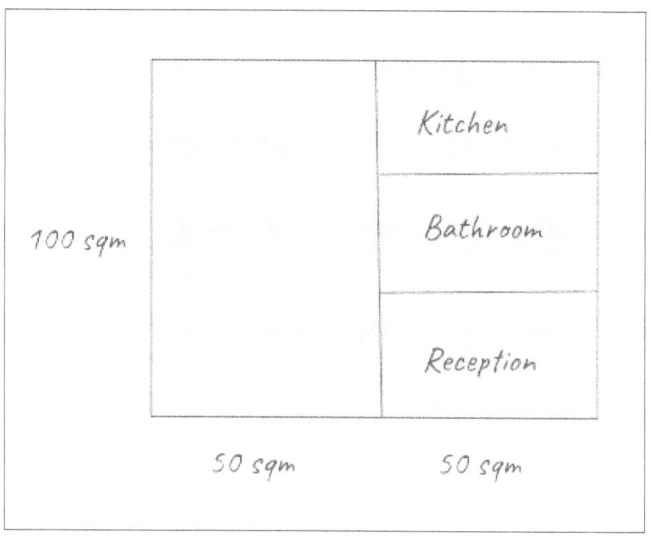

FIGURE 14. While not compulsory, it could help to draw a visual map like the one above to keep track of your assumptions.

Candidate: Let's say 50% of the restaurant will be dedicated to sitting our guests, and the kitchen, bathrooms, reception, and other accessory areas will use the rest. This means that we have an area of 100 square meters that we can use to sit with our guests. As we want a pretty premium restaurant, we cannot put too many tables close to one another, and we will need to leave enough space for the waiters. I am making an assumption and saying that only 20% of the surface will be occupied by the tables. So that would be twenty square meters. We know that each table occupies one square meter, plus we need to consider the space for the chairs. Hence, let's say that each table occupies an area of two square meters. This means we can have twenty tables in our restaurant, seating at least eighty people, which seems realistic.

You must keep track of the assumptions you are making and take a second to check whether the numbers you are getting as a consequence of your assumptions are realistic. Remember to write all of these assumptions on the right of your paper.

Candidate: Now we need to evaluate the average occupancy rate for every turn of our twenty tables, how many turns we do in a day, and how many days we are open in a year. To make things more precise, we should distinguish between weekend days and weekdays and between lunch and dinner. Let's assume that, on average, we have a 70% occupancy rate. So that would be fifty-six people eating on average at every turn. Let's assume we do only two turns, lunch and dinner. That's 112 people daily. Let's say we are open five days a week all year. That is:

$$5 \text{ days} \times 4 \text{ weeks} \times 12 \text{ months} \times 112 \text{ people}$$

...let's round it up to 110 people/day, which equals 26,400 meals annually. We said that each person pays €40, which is €40 × 26,400 meals, which is approximately 1.4M per year.

The candidate is rounding up her calculations. That's acceptable as long as you let your interviewer know. Again, you are not meant to be a human calculator.

Interviewer: Sounds good.

Candidate: Now we need to look at the online sales.

Interviewer: Let's assume that online sales account for 15% of the total sales.

Candidate: That would be 15% × 1.4M, which is 210K annually. 210K + 1.4M = 1.61 M, so our total revenues are 1.61M annually. We need to consider, however, that in Italy, there is a VAT of 22%, so that means that our revenue after VAT will be approximately 1.3M a year.

Interviewer: All right.

Once you are done with revenues, you should move on to costs. **Costs** are divided into **Fixed Costs**, which are the costs that don't change with the volume of your sales (i.e., legal fees, salaries, etc.), and **Variable Costs** that vary with the number of products sold (raw materials, distribution costs. etc.) and that are calculated by multiplying the **no. of units sold ×   their unitary cost.**

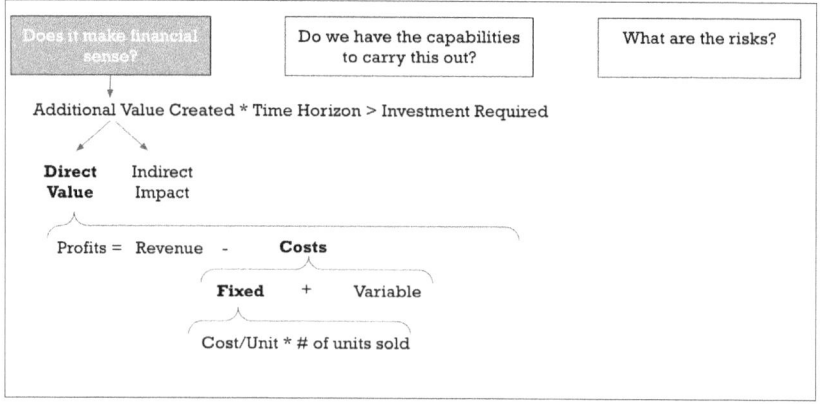

FIGURE 15. This is how the cost side of the equation could be broken down.

Candidate: Now, we need to calculate our costs.

☼ To reduce costs, there are several strategies that you could consider:
Reduce usage of our goods or change with cheaper alternatives
Automate (using technology or implementing a process)
Optimise processes, reducing inefficiencies
Renegotiate existing contracts (to lower procurement costs, for example)

Candidate: Costs are given by the sum of variable costs plus fixed costs. Variable costs are things like the price of the raw material that depends on the quantity sold and are calculated as unitary costs times the number of meals sold, while fixed costs are things like the cost of staff, the cost of bills, and the cost of the rent.

Interviewer: Suppose your variable costs are €25 per meal, and your fixed costs are €15K monthly.

Candidate: Our variable costs are €25 × 26,400 meals per year = €660K. We can then calculate the total costs:

$$Total\ costs = variable\ costs\ (€660K) + fixed\ costs\ (5K \times 12) =$$
$$660K + 180K = 840K$$

Interviewer: Aren't you forgetting something?

Candidate: Humm...you are right. I didn't consider the costs of our online sales. We said before that online sales equals €210K. What's the average order value for online sales?

Interviewer: Let's say €30.

Candidate: Online sales bring us 210K divided by 30, which equals 7K meals more. Is the variable cost per meal the same for online sales as for offline?

Interviewer: Yes.

Watch out for this type of mistake! As mentioned at the beginning of this case, it's important to be clear on the different revenue streams and remember that they will also be reflected in the overall costs.

Candidate: Our variable costs for online sales are 7K × €25, which equals €175K. That means our profits each year before tax will be R (1.3M) - C (840K +175K), which equals 285K. In Italy, profits are taxed at 40%, so our net profits after tax will be 171k. Considering that my friend wanted to receive the investment within three years and that in 3 years, we will be making 171K × 3 = 513K, which is higher than the initial investment of 500K, we can say that opening a restaurant will be financially viable. We made several assumptions that could affect this result, such as the occupancy rate of 70% and the fact that we are open five days a week, doing two turns daily. These seem realistic assumptions; hence, we could address the other two questions. Do we have the capabilities, and what are the risks of such a move?

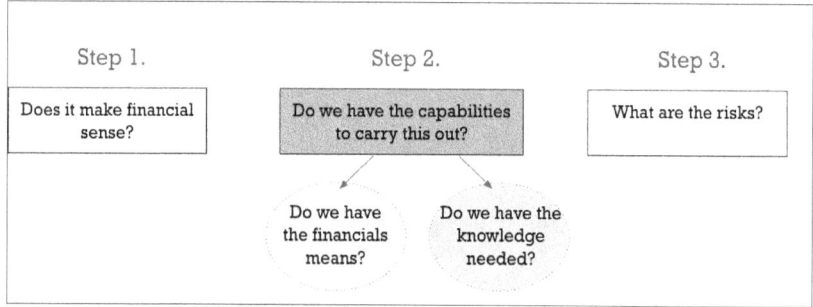

FIGURE 16. When discussing capabilities, we must consider the financial means available and the skills and knowledge required to carry out the task.

Interviewer: What do you have in mind?

Candidate: We must consider if we have the financial capabilities to invest 500K and then support operations for the first six to nine months. I imagine we won't run at full speed in the first months and might have more expenses than income. We will probably need to do some marketing to promote our opening. And then, we must ensure we have the skills and knowledge required to run a restaurant: Who will be the chef? Who will take care of the customers? What if the chef gets sick? Etc... Do we have enough liquidity on top of the initial investment to support operations for the first few months and face any unforeseen event that might come our way?

Interviewer: Yes, we have another 500K in the bank that we can use if needed.

Candidate: That's great to hear. We must also check the knowledge required to run a restaurant and consistently cook a great meal. Does my friend have any experience running a restaurant, and who will do the cooking?

Interviewer: Your friend had a bar just last year that he sold to open this restaurant. He has already contacted a chef who ran a Michelin-starred restaurant in the past and would come on board and be in control of the menu.

Candidate: Sounds great to me!

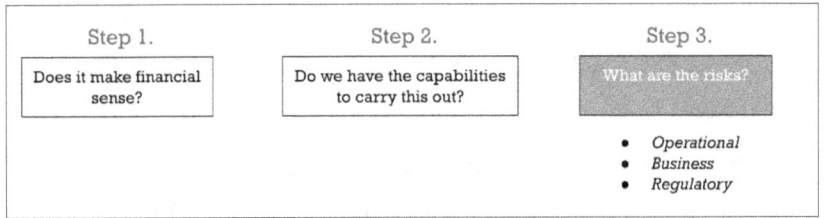

FIGURE 17. When discussing risks, we need to distinguish at least three areas of risk: operational, business-related, and regulatory.

Interviewer: And in terms of risks?

Candidate: We need to consider the business risks, such as the rising prices of raw materials, intense competition, and the possibility of another Thai restaurant opening close to ours or another pandemic hitting. Then there are the operational risks, such as the chef leaving us with no notice or our suppliers needing to deliver the food on time. And the regulatory risks, including the chance that we might not get the license to operate!

Interviewer: Rap it all up for me.

Candidate: Opening a Thai restaurant in the center of Milan with an initial investment of 500K to be covered within three years makes sense if we have at least 20 tables with an occupancy rate of 70% five days a week, twice a day. Assuming the average bill per person is around €40 for offline sales and €30 for online sales, we will recover our initial investment and profit within three years. However, we should consider several other factors, such as whether we have the skills to pull it off and the financial possibilities to sustain our business at least for the first six months. Considering how eager my friend is to start his entrepreneurial activity, I believe these risks will be manageable, and we will be able to find the skills we are missing in the market.

Interviewer: Great, thanks for the recap.

In this case, the problem was about maximizing profits. What happens if you are asked something less business-oriented, such as: "The UN is considering launching a Digital Elementary Program in Zambia. Should they do it?". This is also a Go/No-Go case, and guess what? You will solve it by precisely following the same structure above!

=> **Step 1: What's the core question?** => In this example, it could be an "average increase in the number of students graduating to secondary school."

=> **Step 2: What's the criterion to answer the question?** => 1) Will the number of students graduating reach a certain threshold within the timeframe set by the UN? 2) Do we have the capabilities to implement the program? 3) Are the risks bearable?

=> **Step 3: How can we check if the criterion can be met?** => 1) It will be a matter of comparing the current number of students graduating vs. those we expect to graduate within X years. To do so, we must lay out a structure to understand the variables/drivers that affect the number of students graduating. 2) Do we have the skills to carry this out from a knowledge, political, and financial perspective? 3) What are the risks that we could incur?

As you can see, you can easily apply the same structure to ensure your answers are structured and to the point.

☼ If the question is whether or not to **launch a new product or enter a new market**, remember that there are usually four ways to do so:

1) **Starting from scratch.** This means you consider what it would take for your company to develop a product from scratch or to set up operations in a new market from zero.

2) **Acquisition.** The fastest way to grow profits quickly or to enter a new market is to buy a company that has already done that activity in that particular market.

3) **Joint Venture.** Instead of buying out a company, you might want to do a partnership or joint venture, in which both companies gain something from the new agreement (for example, a % of the new sales generated).

4) **Outsource.** You should always consider outsourcing the development of a new product or opening a new market to a third-party company that could do it for you. It saves you a lot of headaches but eats into your margins!

Note: Check out Chapter 9: question #4. Using the N.A.I.L.E.D. methodology, we have answered a consulting Go/No-Go question in detail.

Consultative			
ESTimation	**Go/No-go**	**Diagnostic**	**Brainstorming**

Example:

- *The profits of company X have been declining. Why?*
- *Amazon's stock valuation has been dropping. What can we do about it?*
- *There has been a slowdown in the Coca-Cola Light segment. What can the management do to solve this issue?*

Here are the three steps you should follow to tackle these questions:

	ESTimation	**Go/No-go**	**Diagnostic**	**Brainstorming**
Step 1.	Elucidate	CONTEXT	**WHAT**	DEFINE
Step 2.	Structure	CRITERION	**WHY**	DISAGGREGATE
Step 3.	Terminate	MEETING THE CRITERION	**HOW**	DEVELOP

To answer these questions, let's go through a real-life interview:

Interview:

Odeon Cinema, the biggest chain of cinemas in Italy, has been experiencing a decline in its margins in the last few years. The management is trying to isolate the cause of this decline. Can you help them brainstorm a solution to get out of this situation?

Here are the three steps you should follow:

=> Step 1: Focus on the WHAT is happening, in particular on the mathematical drive of the problem;

=> Step 2: Move on to the WHY, meaning the cause behind the issue that you have defined in step 1;

=> Step 3: Define HOW you plan to solve the issue;

Let's start from the beginning:

=> Step 1: Focus on the WHAT;

First, you must define the question's objective, ensure it is linked to an operational metric, and understand how it relates to your customer's business model. Then, determine which mathematical variables are causing the issue. We must create a decision tree to spot the issue's root. In this case, the goal will be to analyze the different branches of the tree until it's clear what variables impact the metric. You will need to run a quantitative analysis.

Candidate: If I understood correctly, Odeon is experiencing a decline in its profits. We need to figure out what's happening and develop possible solutions. Is there any other objective I need to be aware of?

Interviewer: Nope, that's it.

Candidate: Can you tell me more about Odeon's business model? How many cinemas do they have, and how do they make money?

Interviewer: Odeon is composed of 100 cinemas, distributed evenly across Italy. Each cinema makes money by selling movie tickets and food and drinks.

Candidate: OK, these are our only two revenue streams, correct?

Interviewer: Indeed.

Candidate: Based on this, let's break down the profits into its different components and try to understand which variables have been impacted.

The candidate draws the following tree:

FIGURE 18. When we analyze the "WHAT" in a diagnostic case, we need to focus on spotting which variables are impacting (from a mathematical perspective) our key objective/metric.

Candidate: Let's start with the revenues. Have revenues declined over the last several years? Which of the two revenue streams have declined, and by how much?

Interviewer: Revenues have been falling by 4% YoY in ticket sales and by 20% in food sales.

The interviewer just gave us some vital information. Since revenues are declining, we need to look deeper into their components. Had the interviewer said that revenues were growing by 10%, we could have asked him about costs to see if that was the origin of the issue. In this case, we need to start from revenues.

FIGURE 19. In this example, the candidate tracks the critical variables and information found along the way while focusing on the metrics that have negatively impacted profits.

Candidate: All right. Let's break down these two metrics, starting with the tickets sold. Sales depend on the average price of tickets × the number of tickets sold. Have both of these metrics declined last year, and if so, by how much? And is this a trend of the previous year alone?

Interviewer: We increased our average prices from €7 to €8 this year, and the number of tickets sold decreased by 20% compared to last year. Revenues have been declining for the previous two years.

Candidate: So, we increased our prices by approx. 14% this year, and the number of tickets sold has decreased by 20%. That means that the demand for our tickets is elastic to the price we set, meaning that the demand is affected proportionally more by a reduction in price. What were our total revenues from this revenue stream last year?

Interviewer: 20M.

Candidate: Our revenue was 20M, and we sold our tickets for 7. That means we sold 20M ÷ 7 = approx. 3M tickets. This year, we increased our prices to 8, and our sales decreased by -20% to 2.4M tickets. This year's revenues from the sales of tickets are 2.4M × €8 = €19.2M, which means that the decrease in the number of tickets sold drives a reduction of approximately 4% in total revenue from ticket sales. The number of tickets sold depends on tickets sold in each cinema per year × the number of cinemas. Did we close any venues?

Interviewer: No, we didn't.

Candidate: Hence, the decrease is due to the number of tickets sold on average per cinema, which depends on the average number of customers that go to each cinema × the number of tickets each customer purchases in a year. Which of these variables decreased?

Interviewer: The average number of tickets per attendee stayed the same.

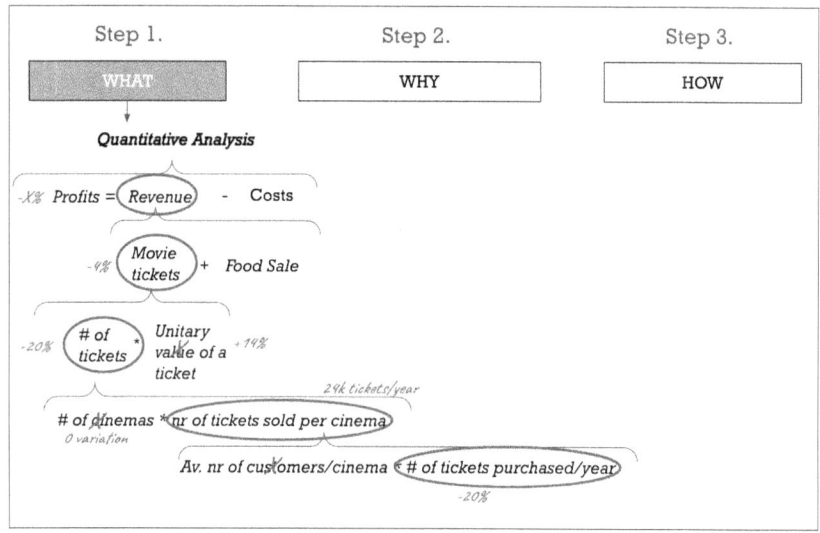

FIGURE 20. And here it is. We can now see which variable has impacted the number of tickets sold and the revenue generated from selling movie tickets, reducing our overall profits.

As you can see, the candidate adheres to the structure and obtains the information needed to understand the variables that have been impacted mathematically.

Candidate: Since the total number of customers attending the cinema stayed the same, we can infer they are going 20% fewer times a year. Before the price change, did the number of tickets sold decrease?

Interviewer: Yes, it did, but by 8%.

Candidate: OK. Let's look at the revenues generated by selling food; what were the revenues last year from this source? Did we change our pricing, and how much did our volume change over the previous years?

Interviewer: Total revenues last year were 30M€. Our pricing stayed the same.

Candidate: OK, so we know that revenue from this source fell by 20% this year, which means a decline of 6M vs last year. Since our pricing didn't change, the revenue decrease is driven by a decline in the number of meals, snacks, and beverages drank before the shows. All of this can be explained by the fact that we have fewer people going to our cinemas.

Candidate: We must analyze the costs before giving you a possible rationale and solution. Did they increase during the last years?

Interviewer: Look at this chart…what does it tell you?

☼ Analyzing graphs or charts is a relatively rare task in tech interviews, but it may be required for some strategy-related roles, particularly during case studies. When presented with a chart, focus on the insights and not just state the obvious. Always relate the chart to the last thing you discussed with the interviewer or the last question and the context of your conversation. This will help you stay focused and avoid getting lost in the data.

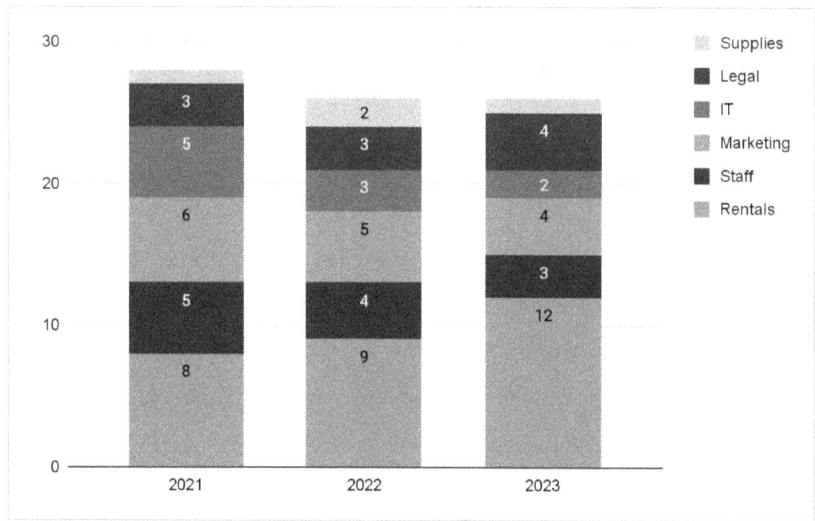

FIGURE 21. Example of a chart that you might be asked to analyze. In this case, the chart shows how total costs and the cost breakdown by department changed over time.

In this case, the temptation could be to start to calculate the variation of each cost category over time or to spend time saying, "We can see the marketing costs reduced while the rental costs have been going up." That would be a waste of time. It's an evident observation. There is no need to point it out. What's the insight here?

If you don't know how to answer this question, ask yourself: What's the context of the case? What was the last thing you talked about with the interviewer before she shared the chart? In this case, we know that margins are falling. We need to find the cause. As you can see from the graph, the total costs haven't changed much over time. They are just slightly lower than in 2021. What does it tell you? **Costs are not the issue.**

Candidate: The total costs have mostly stayed the same over time. There have been some changes in the different components that I can explore further, but I would only focus on this if it would help us solve our issue of margins falling. The issue is clearly on the revenue side: customers are going to our cinemas less.

So, we need to generate more revenue. I need to find a solution to the fall in our revenues rather than focusing on what changed in our overall costs.

Interviewer: OK, what is your next step?

Now that the WHAT is clear, you move on to the WHY.

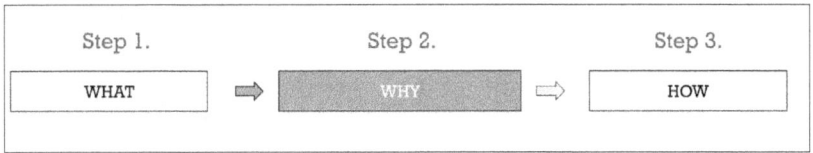

FIGURE 22. Once we are clear about the mathematical drivers impacting our key objective/metric, we should try to understand why these drivers are happening.

Candidate: We need to know why people are going to the cinema less, and the increase in the ticket price could be one reason. Is this reduction in profit something that is happening only to us, or are our competitors experiencing a similar trend?

Interviewer: Only our chain is seeing a sharp margin reduction.

Candidate: Were we the only ones raising the ticket prices?

Interviewer: Indeed.

Candidate: Why did we make that decision?

Interviewer: Our shareholders are getting impatient because revenues are no longer growing. They want to see growth!

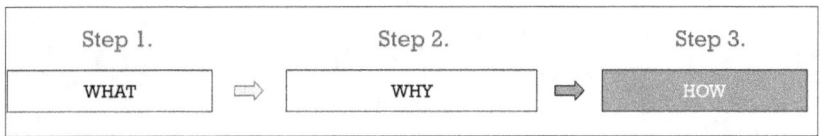

FIGURE 23. The last step in a diagnostic case is brainstorming possible solutions to address the issue.

Now, it's time to move to the HOW phase. Let's brainstorm some solutions. The better, the more original, out-of-the-box, but still grounded options you can develop.

☼ There are many ways to increase your sales. You can focus on the **quantity of products sold or raise prices**.

To increase volumes, you can:

- Add new product lines to sell more to the same or new customers.
- Bundle existing products to make them more appealing.
- Add new distribution channels (online and offline, resellers or partners).
- Focus on the audience segments growing the most or bringing the highest margins.
- Invest in a marketing campaign.
- Adapt your strategy to seasonality.
- Increase market share by acquiring a competitor, doing a joint venture, or merging.
- Focus on new industries with high-entry barriers.
- Focus on technological improvements to boost production and reduce costs.

If you are asked to **change your product prices or pick the product price**, you can set your prices based on the following:

- **Competitors' prices or substitute prices.** (Is there a product that could substitute for yours, even without direct competition? If so, how much does it cost?)
- **Cost-based.** This means you add a margin that you think is sustainable on top of the cost of producing your products. To price a product at the production cost could be a strategy to gain market share and kick out the competition by starting a "price war." However, this strategy is not sustainable in the long term and can only be implemented by companies with big enough cash reserves.

- **Customer-based pricing.** Customers might be willing to pay more than a product costs if it brings them value (enjoyability, impact, or competitive pricing). Think about perfumes or luxury goods. Often, they have a 5x margin over the production costs. In this specific example, the value of luxury, exclusivity, or quality justifies such an uptick over the base cost. Also, consider the additional services you could provide to justify a higher price (i.e., customer support, concierge service, etc.).

Candidate: To solve the case, I would reduce the price of our tickets, possibly creating some buzz around it. I would brainstorm new ways to generate profits without impacting ticket sales. For example, increasing the number of shows per day, having an IMAX screen that could attract new customers and allow us to charge higher prices, opening a restaurant that provides full meals and not just snacks, or buying one of our smaller competitors with solid financials and growth rates. If we have reasonable cash reserves and the current low interest rates, we could also consider buying some real estate to lower our rental costs while taking on cheap debt.

Interviewer: Can you wrap it up for me then?

Candidate: Sure. Our goal was to help a chain of cinemas that saw their profits decline. We understood the issue's root was that customers went to the cinema 20% fewer times a year. This situation has been a direct cause of an increase in ticket prices by +14%, which caused a disproportionate reduction in ticket sales. We proposed several options that did not force us to reduce ticket sales to address the issue and ensure our stakeholders are happy with the new growth.

Consultative			
ESTimation	**Go/No-go**	**Diagnostic**	**Brainstorming**

Example:

- *The government of South Africa wants to launch a new education program to help reduce the illiteracy rate among kids below 15 years old. How would you help them set up this program? In which ways could we achieve X?*

Here are the three steps you should follow to tackle these types of questions:

	ESTimation	Go/No-go	Diagnostic	**Brainstorming**
Step 1.	Elucidate	CONTEXT	WHAT	**DEFINE**
Step 2.	Structure	CRITERION	WHY	**DISAGGREGATE**
Step 3.	Terminate	MEETING THE CRITERION	HOW	**DEVELOP**

To answer these questions, let's go through a real-life interview:

Interviewer:

A guitar manufacturer seeks to quadruple its profits in four years, and they asked our help to set up a strategy to achieve this goal.

=> Step 1: Define the question and its operational focus metric and get the context.

=> Step 2: Disaggregate the questions into their drivers and spot the levers we can influence.

=> Step 3: Come up with ideas to solve the issue.

Let's start from:

=> Step 1: Define the question, its operational focus metric and clarify the context;

In this case, the focus metric is straightforward: increase profits.

Candidate: To summarize, our client is a guitar producer who needs our help to quadruple their profits in 4 years. Correct? Is there any other objective I should know about?

Interviewer: They want to protect their brand image at all costs.

Candidate: Can you tell me more about what they are afraid of from a branding perspective?

Interviewer: They want to boost their profits, but not if it means selling a lower quality product or reducing the level of service provided to their current customers.

Interviewer: OK, clear. Please tell me more about their business. How do they generate revenue? Where do they sell? How are they positioned in the market?

Interviewer: They are an American company that sells in the US only but has a powerful and recognized brand. They are a premium guitar manufacturer focused on acoustic and electric guitars. They own many stores in different states and then distribute their product through resellers to other music stores. They have also just launched an e-commerce store.

Candidate: OK. Why do they want to quadruple their profits in four years?

Interviewer: Because they would like to go public in four years. The higher the profits, the higher the valuation.

Candidate: What are their current revenue and profit? How have they been trending in the last three years?

Interviewer: $100M in revenue and $5M in profits. Profits have been flat during the past few years.

Candidate: How is the overall industry doing? And our competitors?

Interviewer: The musical instrument industry is growing, mainly thanks to all the digital devices linked to electronic music production. Our competitors are Yamaha and Fender; they own 60% of the guitar market. They are growing at 10% YoY.

Candidate: And in terms of profits, how are they doing?

Interviewer: Yamaha generated 600M in revenue and 50M in profits last year, while Fender generated 500M and 20M in profits. Both have had flat profits for the previous few years.

Candidate: So, our competition isn't growing either. How are we positioned in the market? Are we a luxury brand?

Interviewer: We are a luxury brand. We are, on average, 20% more expensive than Yamaha and Fender.

Now that you have some crucial info regarding the company you are working for (goals, revenue streams, positioning in the market, distribution channels), you understand the context (industry trends and the competition), you can move ahead to the second step.

=> Step 2: Disaggregate the questions into its drivers and spot the levers;

Of course, you could break down profits into each component (revenue and costs) and see how to increase or decrease each. This approach would be correct, but it would lack originality.

When brainstorming questions, we suggest looking at the big picture, starting by understanding whether there are different ways to generate profits that still need to be explored.

You can increase profits by focusing on existing activities or opening new revenue streams.

Candidate: Our goal is to increase profits, which have stagnated for the past few years. We could focus on generating more profits from our existing business or finding new profit streams. If we focus on existing activities, we could consider selling our products in new markets or selling more of our products in existing ones.

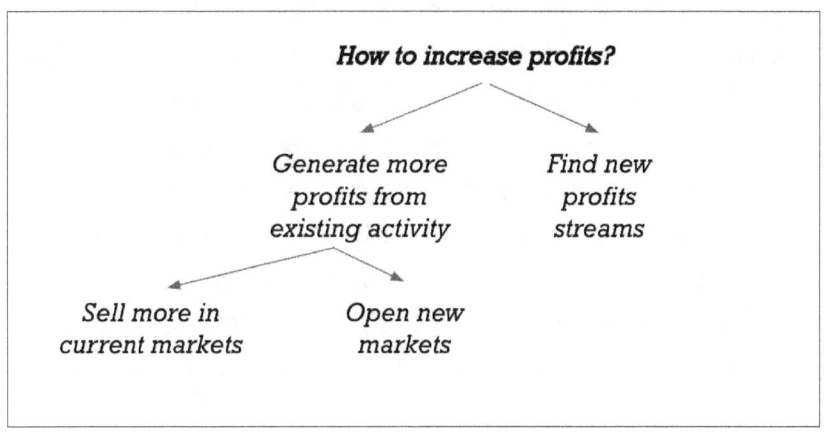

FIGURE 24. Profits can be increased by either focusing on what we currently have/what we are presently doing or by trying to open up a new channel to generate profits.

Candidate: To increase profits in our current markets, focusing only on our existing activities, we can invest in marketing activities, sign new distribution agreements, or invest more in our e-commerce store to sell more online. Alternatively, we can focus on pricing by developing new designs and using high-quality materials or raise our prices if demand is not sensitive to price changes. We can also optimize our fixed and variable costs to reduce expenses. Alternatively, we can explore new markets where we are not currently active or open up new revenue streams to increase our profits.

=> Step 3: Develop ideas on influencing the levers to address the core question.

Interviewer: How would you enter new markets or create new revenue streams?

Candidate: To explore new markets, we could develop a market prioritization map to identify a few markets that have the highest potential for us. We could consider factors such as market size, existing competition, barriers to entry, distribution channels, and product-market fit. We could rate each aspect from one to five for each market and choose the highest score. We should tackle one market at a time to minimize risks and increase focus. Additionally, you mentioned that the music industry is growing due to the increasing use of digital devices for producing electronic music. In light of this, we could enter this sector by launching our line of digital devices. Alternatively, we could partner with an electronic music producer to develop an innovative product to disrupt this market. Despite competition in this sector, we could leverage our strong brand recognition to gain traction quickly. Lastly, we could consider acquiring a minor player with an existing customer base and product in this sector. We must evaluate each option to determine swiftly which will yield the desired result with the lowest risks and resources required.

With this example, we have completed all the different types of consulting cases that you might have to face. Bear in mind:

1) A case could require a mix of approaches (Go/No-Go and Brainstorming, for example);

2) Now it's time to practice! You will find many more sample consulting cases on our website: Gogotechy.com.

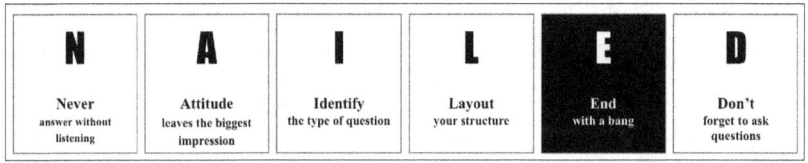

5) END WITH A BANG

As you have seen, it's standard for the interviewer to ask you to summarize your findings during consultative questions. However, remember to end with a summary for every question. It's essential to show that you are in control of the narrative and the information shared and that you can recap them in less than a minute so they can stick in the minds of your future customers.

When you recap your answer, the goal is to:

a) Highlight the fundamental assumptions that you made and how changing them could impact your final answer;

b) Share your considerations and insights on the findings;

c) Recap your answer with a clear "yes or no"; it shouldn't be a "probably, maybe, chances are."

Let's end with a bang on the consultative case we saw in the previous section.

Interviewer: Could you summarize your answer for me?

Candidate: We have been asked to help a guitar manufacturer increase profits. The manufacturer is a premium brand, with 100M in revenues and 5M in profit, operating in an industry that is growing. We should consider two paths to boost our earnings: 1) Evaluate new ways of generating profits. For example, by launching a new product into a new market category; 2) increasing our profits by focusing on our existing business activities. In this second case, we must consider entering new markets while selling the same products or optimizing our current business through operations, increasing revenues, or reducing costs. Since our competitors haven't been experiencing an increase in profits either, there is a chance that the guitar industry is saturated. Hence, it could be hard to optimize our business further. A quicker way to achieve our goal is to open a new revenue stream by entering a new segment by creating a new product from scratch or finding a partner. Of these two options, I suggest picking a partner to develop a new product. A partnership could be less capital-intensive and risky, allowing us to pivot our strategy without too many headaches if we realize the electronic market is too competitive or complex.

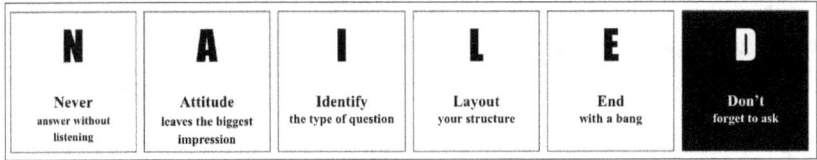

6) DON'T FORGET TO ASK QUESTIONS!

At the end of any interview, it's common practice that the interviewer will leave five to ten minutes for you to ask questions. This might seem trivial, but don't be mistaken! **If you ask irrelevant questions that don't bring any value to the conversation, you might lose points...if not lose the job!** So many candidates didn't pass Google's or Meta's interviews because they closed the interviews with statements by not asking questions or only about health insurance.

Asking questions allows you to learn more about the role, the team, your manager, your objectives, or the KPIs you will be measured by. A few examples of good ending questions are:

- *"What are the biggest challenges facing the company right now?"*
  - This question shows that you are interested in the company's long-term success.
- *"What is the company's culture like?"*
  - This question will help you understand the company's values and how you would fit in.
- *"What are the company's goals for the next year?"*
  - This question shows that you are ambitious and looking for a company where you can grow and develop.
- *"What is the company's training and development program like?"*
  - This question shows that you are committed to your professional development and looking for a company to invest in.
- *"Any feedback on my interview so I can improve for the next steps?"*

You can also ask questions specific to the job. For example, if you are interviewing for a marketing position, you could ask questions about the company's marketing strategy or target audience.

Finally, here are a few tips on how close an interview:

1. Thank the interviewer for their time. This is a simple but meaningful gesture that shows your gratitude.

2. Restate your interest in the position. It's your chance to reiterate why you are a good fit for the job.

3. Ask about the next steps. This will show that you are eager to hear back from the company.

4. Follow up with a thank-you note. This is a great way to reiterate your interest in the position and to leave a lasting impression.

Here are some examples of closing statements:

- *"Thank you for your time today. I enjoyed learning more about the position and the company. I have the skills and experience you seek. I am excited about the opportunity to join your team."*

- *"I am very interested in the position and would be a valuable asset to your team. I am eager to hear back from you about the next steps."*

- *"Thank you for your time and consideration. I look forward to hearing from you soon."*

It is essential to be sincere and enthusiastic when you close an interview. This is your chance to make a final impression and leave the interviewer wanting to learn more.

RECAP OF OUR METHODOLOGY.

You now know how to tackle any questions that can come your way. Let's try to summarize everything you have learned so far.

N

NEVER answer without listening.

Use the mirroring technique to ask questions before jumping straight into an answer. You should gather as much information as possible before jumping to any conclusion.

A

ATTITUDE leaves the biggest impression.

Show the right attitude (summarized by S.O.F.T.E.N.) and clarify why you want the specific role you are applying to and nothing else.

I

IDENTIFY the type of question you are being asked.

There are different types of questions, and each requires a different approach. In particular, you could be asked culture-fit questions (personal experience and behavioral questions). Or you could be posed logical questions (general cognitive analysis or consultative questions). Consultative questions can be divided into market sizing, go/no-go, diagnostic, and brainstorming. Whatever the question, your answers should be structured, logical, concise, and engaging.

L

LAYOUT your structure.

The questions above can be answered by laying out a three-step approach. The first step will always be understanding the question's goal and context better. The last step will always be about laying out your rationale by leveraging the information you gathered.

E
END with a bang.
Always summarize your findings. Don't just recap the critical information you gathered; highlight the key assumptions you made and share your insights and considerations.

D
DON'T forget to ask questions.
Always ask questions at the end of an interview to learn more about the company, the role, or your interviewer's experience.

Chapter 9

HOW TO APPLY THE NAILED METHODOLOGY
(TO FOUR COMMON INTERVIEW QUESTIONS)

"I always did something I was a little not ready to do. I think that's how you grow. When there's that moment of 'Wow, I'm not really sure I can do this,' and you push through those moments, that's when you have a breakthrough.[26]"

—Marissa Mayer was the first female software engineer at Google and the former CEO of Yahoo.

- Marissa was born into a middle-class family but had an unwavering drive to succeed. She enrolled at Stanford University to become a doctor but realized medicine wasn't her true passion. She pursued computer science to learn how to solve problems and understand people's thought processes.

- After completing her studies, Marissa received an offer from McKinsey to work as a consultant. However, she also received an email from a headhunter about a new startup called Google. Despite calculating that Google only had a 2 percent chance of succeeding, Marissa was impressed with the quality of the

26 Toren, M. (2014, July 17). Marissa explains it all: 5 motivating quotes from Yahoo's CEO. Entrepreneur. https://www.entrepreneur.com/growing-a-business/marissa-explains-it-all-5-motivating-quotes-from-yahoos/234222

other 19 employees at Google and decided to take the risk. She believed that trying to build a company, regardless of whether it failed or succeeded, would help her learn more.

- As Google's 20th employee, Marissa played a significant role in developing some of the company's most important products, including designing Google's homepage and developing Gmail and Google Maps. She eventually became a senior vice president, with thousands of employees reporting to her and billions of users worldwide using products she helped build. Her job made her worth hundreds of millions of dollars.

- However, Marissa's career at Google hit a snag when Larry Page returned as CEO in 2010. Some critics speculate that their past romantic relationship caused Page to avoid favoritism. Others suggest that Marissa's management style created friction with colleagues. Regardless, Marissa left Google after 13 years to become the CEO of Yahoo. Her main goal was to revive the struggling company, which had lost billions of dollars in revenue and top talent to competitors like Google and Facebook. Unfortunately, Yahoo had to be sold in 2016 at a fraction of its highest valuation.

Let's apply the NAILED Methodology to 4 common questions you could encounter during your interview process to see it in action.

#QUESTION NR.1 - PERSONAL EXPERIENCE:

"Tell me about a time you solved a complex problem."

Context: You are applying for a BDR role at Amazon Web Services.

- **N: Nailing with the right attitude.** You clarify that you want this job and nothing else, and you show through the interview that you are motivated, passionate, and committed to getting this role.

- **A: Ask questions only after listening.** Start by repeating the question:

  > *Candidate: OK, you would like me to share an example of when I solved a complex problem. Are you only interested in job-related issues, or can I share examples from passion projects and other non-job situations.? Is there anything else I should address with my answer?*

  At this point, the interviewer might take different directions. We recommend sticking to work-related examples even if they say you can bring up any example. Listen to the interviewer's directions and keep asking questions until you understand what the interviewer expects.

  > *Interviewer: You can share any relevant example. I'd like you to share details about your thought process, how you solved your problem, and what steps you took to address the issue.*

- **I: Identify the type of question.**

  In this case, it's clear that it's a personal experience question, and hence, you can solve it in three steps:

  > Step 1: Identify the real goal of the question;
  >
  > Step 2: Pick a relevant example from your story bank;
  >
  > Step 3: Structure the answer using the S.T.A.R. framework.

- **L: Layout your structure.**

Starting from **Step 1: Identify the real goal of the question** and assess at what point of the interview this question is arriving. Is this the interviewer's first personal experience question, or is it already the third or fourth? If the interviewer has been asking many personal experience questions, they are doubting whether or not you have the right profile and experience for the job. If so, you must ensure that your following answer will be directly linked to the job.

Step 2: Pick a relevant example from your story bank. Prepare at least five examples from your past experiences that you can adapt to any behavioral or personal experience question. Let's imagine that one of the examples you had prepared was about your previous work experience when you were given a monthly target as a BDR that seemed impossible to achieve. It would help if you tweaked the answer to showcase that you have an excellent selling attitude and know how to close a customer. Ask the interviewer for a minute or two to prepare your answer. Write down a few keywords to help you remember the key concepts you want to get across for every letter of the S.T.A.R. framework.

Step 3: Use the S.T.A.R. framework to structure your answer.

- **Situation:** In one minute, explain to the interviewer the problem you were facing.

  Candidate: In my previous job, I worked as a BDR for the Public Sector team at Hubspot. We sold a SaaS solution to governments and other public entities. I was part of a 10-BDR team focusing on the French market.

- **Task:** What goal were you working toward? Which task did you have to carry out?

Candidate: As soon as I finished my ramp-up, which lasted approximately one month, I was given an ACV [annual contractual value] target of $2M a quarter and was asked to generate at least 10 SAOs [sales accepted opportunities] per week. Talking with other fellow BDRs who had started more or less with me and who had the same level of seniority, I realized that my target was double what they had. It was an impossible target to achieve.

○ **Action:** Describe the actions you took to address the situation with an appropriate amount of detail and keep the focus on YOU.

Candidate: The first thing I did was sit down with my manager to get his point of view and suggestions on the best way to tackle this task. In particular, I asked him if he had any tips or suggestions on which vertical, type of account, or product to focus on to reduce the average sales cycle as much as possible. I then sat down with the best BDRs in the Public Sector team in EMEA to understand what they were doing to achieve the results they were given. I tried to learn how they were prospecting new leads, to whom they were speaking within the target accounts, and which content or material they were sharing with customers. I then laid out a go-to-market plan involving my account executives. I worked with them to define a lead list and give each lead a priority score to understand which were the hottest leads, to contact first, and which were the coldest to reach last.

○ **Result:** Describe the outcome of your actions. Don't be shy about taking credit for your behavior.

Candidate: It wasn't easy, but thanks to this prep work, I felt I had a clear action plan fully supported by my key stakeholders. I started the outreach activity and closed my first quarter with a 105% revenue overachievement and 140% SAOs generated.

- **E: End with a bang.**

  Candidate: To recap, my problem when I started my first quarter as a BDR at HubSpot was that I was given a target twice as high as the ones of other BDRs of my same tenure. Nonetheless, after learning the best practices, I developed a clear go-to-market strategy, setting clear priorities and a clear action plan. Thanks to this work and involving my critical stakeholders, I could smash my ACV and activity quota.

- **D: Don't forget to ask questions.** If this were the last question of your interview, now would be a good time to ask questions about the job, the company, your manager's experience, or the team's goals.

#QUESTION NR.2 - BEHAVIOURAL EXPERIENCE:

"You have just joined a new team. After one week on the job, you have noticed a lot of tension between two of your colleagues. How would you handle this situation?"

Context: You are applying for the program manager position at Apple.

- N: Nailing with the right attitude. Clarify that you want this job and nothing else. Show that you are motivated, passionate, and committed to getting this role.

- A: Ask questions only after listening.

  Candidate: If I understood correctly, I am new to the team. After only one week, I saw that some issues affected the relationship between two of my colleagues. You want to know how I would handle this delicate situation. Is there anything else you would like me to focus on?

  Interviewer: Do you think it's part of your role to fix these issues? Is there any other objective you can think of?

  Candidate: Well, I am new to the team. I don't know much about the company's culture, the history between these two people, and how many managers like handling these situations. Let's say that there are many incognita. But I do believe that a team's success depends on the health of the overall work environment, and it's everyone's responsibility to ensure people get along. So, I guess my objective is to resolve this issue as quickly as possible so we can focus on doing what's best for the team, the company, and our customers.

  Candidate: Am I the only one who noticed this issue? Is this situation affecting the team's performance or morale?

  Interviewer: Your colleagues have been aware of this but haven't done anything about it for a while. The situation is impacting the team's morale.

  Candidate: Is the manager or HR aware?

Ask your interviewer questions for a few minutes to get your thinking straight.

- **I: Identify the type of question.** In this case, it's a behavioral experience question. You can solve it in three steps:

  > Step 1: Identify the real goal of the question;
  >
  > Step 2: Pick one of your pre-created examples;
  >
  > Step 3: Structure the answer using the S.T.A.R. framework.

- **L: Layout your structure.**

  Start with **Step 1, Identify the real goal of the question.** Why is the interviewer asking you this question? Which behaviors, values, or skills should you get across? Remember that some of Apple's values are: "Looking ahead for Apple, looking out for all" and "A healthy respect for well-being." You should focus your answer so that it will be evident that you have the well-being of your colleagues front and center, that you are a team player, that you care about people, and that you are proactive about solving problems head-on.

  Step 2: Pick one of your pre-created examples. You may be tempted to answer the question as if it was a theoretical exercise. While this wouldn't be wrong, it would weaken your answer. Is there any example you can use from your past that is similar to this situation and can be used to showcase how you tackled such a problem? If yes, bring it up.

  Step 3: Use the START framework to structure your answer.

  - **Situation:** Remember to keep the background short.

    Candidate: I have found myself in a similar situation in the past. I had just changed jobs within my previous company, and I noticed a sour relationship between one of my colleagues working as an Account Executive and his Solution Engineer.

  - **Task:** What goal were you working toward? What was your role?

Candidate: While their relationship wasn't impacting my job per se, it affected the overall relationship between the two teams. For this reason, I felt it was vital to take action and improve the situation.

○ **Action:** Describe the actions you took to address the situation with an appropriate amount of detail and keep the focus on you.

Candidate: To help tackle the situation, I sat down with my colleague and the engineer separately, discussing the topic and trying to get their point of view. I then brought up the situation to my manager and shared the conflicting views and the reasons for the quarrel. I suggested organizing a meeting for the two of them to explain the reasons for their conflict and offered my help as a mediator.

○ **Result:** Describe the outcome of your actions, and don't be shy about taking credit for your behavior.

Candidate: My manager took the suggestion, we organized the meeting, and both employees finally had a frank conversation about why they were so tense and gave each other feedback on where to improve.

- **E: End with a bang.**

  Candidate: In this case, I would apply a similar approach, first trying to understand what's going on, then involving my manager to get her feedback and establish a plan, and then I would offer my help to organize a meeting and set up a transparent and honest team culture.

- **D: Don't forget to ask questions.** If this were the last question of your interview, now would be a good time to ask questions.

#QUESTION NR.3: - GCA

"Give me an example of how you would create a strategy to increase revenue per game at a bowling alley."

Context: You are applying for an Account Manager role at Google.

- **N: Nail the interview with the right attitude.** Always want the job first and the company second.

- **A: Ask questions only after listening.** Ask the recruiter some follow-up questions:

  > *Candidate: You would like me to develop a strategy to increase the revenue generated on every game at a bowling alley. Is there any other objective I should know about?*

  > *Interviewer: No, that's pretty much it.*

  > *Candidate: Do you want me to focus just on revenues or on overall profits as well?*

  > *Interviewer: Only revenues.*

  > *Candidate: Is there any reason you wish to increase revenue alone, apart from making more money?*

  > *Interviewer: Our costs have increased due to higher energy prices and inflation. These are eating into our margins, and we need to figure out how to increase our revenue if we want to stay afloat.*

  > *Candidate: OK, clear.*

  Ask your interviewer for a couple of minutes to get your thinking straight.

- **I: Identify the type of question.** In this case, it's clear that it's a question, and hence, you can solve it in three steps:

  > Step 1: Clarify;

  > Step 2: Structure;

  > Step 3: Explain.

- **L: Layout your structure.**

Starting from **Step 1: Clarify and dig into** the context and the goal. What's the issue that you have been facing, and how will success be measured? Then, figure out who is involved, who you need to work with, and which resources or limitations you should consider before proposing a solution.

Here is an example of how you could do it:

> *Candidate: Let me recap to see if I got all the information correct. We are a bowling alley; our profits have decreased due to rising energy costs and inflation. Hence, we want to increase the revenue generated on every game. If we don't, we might run out of business. Do we have any liquidity left? Can I develop new investment ideas, or do we only need to solve the problem with our current resources?*
>
> *Interviewer: $50K left in our account, and then we run out of money.*
>
> *Candidate: OK, so we are pretty tight on the money! First, I would like to understand more about the operating context. How are we doing compared to our competitors? Has there been any change we need to be aware of in the market? Then, I want to dive deep into our company, how we generate money, how we attract new customers, and where we are investing. Finally, I want to outline a few ideas for increasing revenues while saving money.*
>
> *Interviewer: Sounds good.*
>
> *Candidate: How many bowling alleys are there in Paris? Is it trendy, or is this a declining sector?*
>
> *Interviewer: The number of alleys is pretty stable, but a new alley opened 5km from here. It's brand new and bigger. They offer pretty much the same services that we do and at the same price.*
>
> *Candidate: Do you think they are stealing our clients?*
>
> *Interviewer: Not yet, but they might.*

Candidate: How are we differentiating ourselves from them?

Interviewer: We aren't. We have just been around for longer.

Candidate: Did anything happen in the market that we should be aware of? Is there any new technology or trend?

Interviewer: There is a digitalization process happening. All venues are adding screens and digital elements to the customer experience. We renovated our facility two years ago, so it is up-to-date.

Candidate: OK, let's move on to understand our company better. How big is it? Where is it located? How is the business going? What are the current revenue streams?

Interviewer: We are a medium-sized bowling alley with ten lanes, a bar, and a small video game area. We are located south of Paris, just outside the city center. The business is going quite well, meaning our customer inflow is stable, and there is a reasonable rate of returning customers. The primary revenue streams are people bowling and alcohol consumption at the bar.

Candidate: How many people can play simultaneously on a lane, and how long is the game on average?

Interviewer: Up to six people and lanes are booked in one-hour slots.

Candidate: Hence, we could have sixty people playing simultaneously every hour. How much do customers pay to play?

Interviewer: €10 an hour

Candidate: We could generate €600 an hour at total capacity. When are we open?

Interviewer: Monday to Saturday, from 3 pm to 11 pm.

Candidate: We are open eight hours daily, six days a week, but not on Sundays. Is this the norm?

Interviewer: No, this is entirely discretionary. The owner didn't want to work on Sundays when you have to pay more for staff. Some other alleys stay open until 1 am and are usually open on Sundays.

Candidate: OK, if we were at total capacity every hour, we could generate €600 times 8 hours a day times 6 days equals €28,800 a week times 4 weeks equals €130K a month or €1.5M a year. What was our revenue last year? Has it decreased in the previous three years?

Interviewer: We generated approximately €250K a year, half from the bowling and half from the bar. Revenue has been flat for the last three years, with no significant changes.

Candidate: This means that we are generating 125K from the matches out of the 1.5M we could develop if we were at top capacity at all times. It means we generated only 8% of what we could do. How about our profits? You mentioned that they have been declining. What's our current profit margin?

Interviewer: We are not making any profit.

Candidate: You mean we are losing money?

Interviewer: No, it means that our income equals our total costs. So, zero profits.

Candidate: Interesting. Who is our customer base?

Interviewer: Most clients are teenagers between sixteen and twenty-one years old. During the week, we have groups of older people passionate about bowling, usually between 6 pm to 10 pm. These are our most loyal customers, of course.

Candidate: You mentioned that we have a reasonable rate of people returning to play. What's the percentage of new customers vs. returning customers?

Interviewer: Approximately 60% of our customers are returning.

Candidate: Is this a good metric for a place like ours?

Interviewer: It's pretty much aligned with the competition.

Candidate: How are we attracting new customers, and how are we retaining them?

Interviewer: We are not doing any particular marketing activity. We have a website where customers can book their slot, and we offer a 5% discount to returning customers on their next match.

Candidate: You mentioned that half of the revenue comes from the bar. What are we selling? What's our top seller?

Interviewer: We sell only beers and soft drinks. We offer no meals, only snacks. Heineken is the top seller.

Candidate: Do we serve only one brand of beer? Why don't we serve meals?

Interviewer: Yes, only Heineken. We only have one person taking care of the bar, and it wouldn't be possible for this person also to make cocktails and prepare food.

Candidate: We never thought of hiring someone else to do this job.

Interviewer: Yes, of course. But we didn't want to add additional costs.

Candidate: I see. How many employees do we have in total?

Interviewer: We have 6: one bartender, a receptionist, a manager, and 3 waiters.

Step 2: Lay out your structure.

In a GCA question, your structure should be:

1. Recap key intel;

2. State your recommendation;

3. Explain your rationale.

Let's see it in action!

[Recap key intel]

> *Candidate: OK, let me take a minute to recap what we have learned so far. We are a medium-sized, renovated bowling alley with ten alleys in central Paris. We operate in a stagnant sector and have a more significant, newer, brighter competitor 5km away. We generate 250K a year, half coming from the tickets and the other half selling soft drinks and beers, generating no profits. Our audience is either teenagers or older folks during the week. We are closed on Sundays, while the other days are open eight hours. We don't do any marketing, and we have an average return rate of 60% of our customers and an occupancy rate of just 8%.*

[State your recommendation]

> *Candidate: Based on this information, my recommendation is to increase the venue's overall occupancy, attract new customers, and maximize every opportunity to generate additional revenue. We can do so by opening new revenue streams, differentiating ourselves from the competition, and expanding our customer base.*

[Explain the rationale]

> *Candidate: We need to maximize our potential. If we don't act quickly to differentiate ourselves, we will lose all our customers. To do that, I suggest using 35K of our 50K to hire one more person to focus on food preparation to create a new revenue stream, something that our competition cannot copy easily. We could start, for example, with "hamburgers & margaritas night" or "fish and chips bowling day" during the week to increase the occupancy rate during the slower days. These meals are easy to prepare, generate high margins, and help us create buzz to attract new customers. We could also start to offer local artisanal beers. I am sure there are plenty of local brands that would be keen to have access to our customer base. We should start organizing tournaments to develop*

a sense of community and make the most out of the older crowd. We could push this new offering through digital and offline marketing campaigns. We should also consider opening on Sundays and staying closed on Mondays and Tuesdays when people have less time to play. Considering that half of the audience are teenagers, we should consider what they like. It could make sense to take advantage of the video game area and lease some arcade video games, ping-pong tables, or pool tables. Finally, I would consider adding a subscription model. Allowing people to buy an early subscription at a discounted price will incentivize them to come more frequently and spend more at the bar or on food while reducing the risk of them leaving to the competition.

- **E: End with a bang.**

    Candidate: We have 50K in the bank and need to make it count to increase our revenues; otherwise, we will have to succumb to the competition. Our goal should be to differentiate ourselves as much as possible and to improve the overall occupancy rate by incentivizing our customers to come during the week and maximizing weekends. I would introduce subscriptions, open on Sundays, hire someone dedicated to preparing easy meals and cocktails, and invest in organic and paid marketing activities to attract new customers.

#QUESTION NR.4 - CONSULTING GO/NO-GO:

"You are the new VP of Strategy at Stripe and have been asked to decide whether or not to enter the Chinese market. How would you make this decision?"

Context: you are applying for an Account Executive role at Stripe.

- **N: Nailing with the right attitude."** As per above, let's assume you have covered this part.

- **A: Ask questions only after listening.** Here, the best way to apply this principle would be to ask the recruiter a series of questions:

> *Candidate: To summarize, the goal is to define whether or not we should enter China. Is there any other objective I should be aware of?*
>
> *Interviewer: I would like to understand which factors you would consider in making this decision and your final suggestion.*
>
> *Candidate: What is our goal? Why are we considering such a decision?*
>
> *Interviewer: We want to ensure we don't lose market share to our competitors who have already entered this massive market, and we want to maximize profits.*
>
> *Candidate: How do you define market share?*
>
> *Interviewer: In this case, it is the weight of our profits compared to the overall profits generated by all the companies active in the payment processing industry.*
>
> *Candidate: Why are we interested in defending our market share?*
>
> *Interviewer: Because the market is becoming very competitive, we are losing our competitive advantage.*
>
> *Candidate: OK, is there any other objective I should know?*
>
> *Interview: No, that's it.*

- **I: Identify the type of question.** In this case, it's clear that it's a consulting question and that it's also a go/no-go case. Hence, you can solve it in three steps:

  > **Step 1:** Identify the real goal of the question.

  > **Step 2:** What's the criterion to answer the question?

  > **Step 3:** How can we check that the criterion has been answered?

  Ask your interviewer for a couple of minutes to get your thinking straight.

- **L: Layout your structure.**

  Step 1: Identify the real goal of the question.

  You've mostly covered this with the intro questions. However, remember the context in which the question was being asked. You are applying for an Account Executive role at Stripe. They are asking this question not because they want you to give the answer that a McKinsey consultant would provide but to make sure you can think logically, with a specific structure, and clearly explain a complex topic. Don't overcomplicate things. Focus on your analytical thinking and storytelling skills.

  Step 2: What's the criterion?

  First, entering China needs to be financially viable. Stripe must have the capabilities (capital and skill) to carry out this operation. Finally, several risks must be considered (legal barriers, political headwinds, unfair competition). If we can face those risks and everything else is in check, your final answer should be a go!

  Step 3: How do we make sure we meet the criterion?

  For this operation to make financial sense, the following formula needs to be true:

Value Added × Time Horizon > Investment Needed

Remember to mention that direct and indirect value will be created (e.g., by entering a new market, you might get a positive impact, such as access to more customers, a positive branding impact, and higher spending from your existing customers).

Candidate: Our goal is to maximize profits and increase our market share. Entering the Chinese market will only help us achieve these objectives if certain conditions are met. In particular, the profits generated within our target time frame should be higher than the investments needed. Then, we should ensure we can carry this move out from a financial and knowledge perspective and evaluate the risks attached. If the risks are worth it and the previous two conditions are met, we should enter China. If not, then it's a no-go. Does that make sense so far?

Interviewer: Yes, it does. So, where do we start?

Candidate: We should start by understanding whether or not this move makes financial sense. If it doesn't, there is no point in going forward. Could you share the time horizon we have to recover our investment and the investment needed for such a move?

Interview: We want to recover our investment in three years. To enter the market, we may need $500M.

Candidate: Thanks. The first condition is that the profits generated by operating in China during the first three years should be higher than $500M. If not, then the operation will not make financial sense. We now need to calculate our potential profits. Profits are the difference between revenues and costs. I will start by analyzing our revenues. Please could you share more information regarding how we plan to generate profits? I understand that Stripe generates money by charging a commission of approx. 3% of every purchase through the *website uses its payment processing technology. Is there any other revenue stream that I should consider?*

Interviewer: Let's focus only on this one.

Candidate: To estimate the revenue generated, I need to calculate the average commission of 3% times the number of transactions we will process. This amount will depend on our customers, the average number of transactions per day per customer, and the average transaction value.

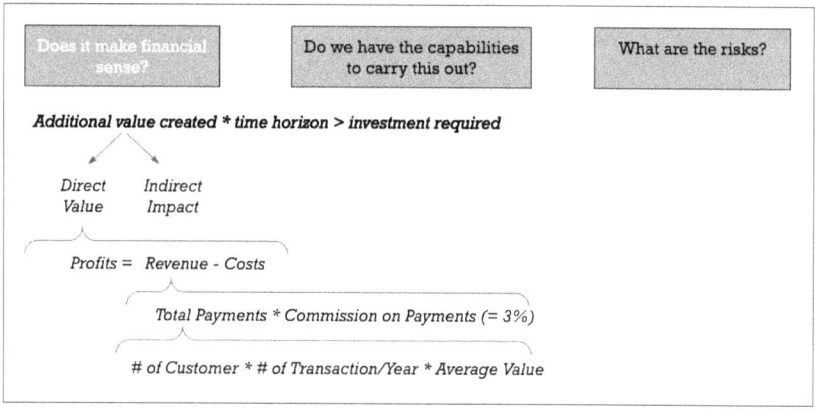

Candidate: To determine the number of customers, do we know the total addressable market in China?

Interviewer: You are overcomplicating things. The e-commerce industry in China generates $100BN in transactions every year.

Candidate: I would assume that in the first year, we will only be able to capture 0.1% of the existing market (= 100M), then in the second year, we will be able to reach 0.5% (500M), then in the third year 1% (1B). Now, I need to understand the costs, both fixed and variable.

Interviewer: Suppose costs are estimated to be 60% of the revenue generated.

Candidate: Perfect. This means that my costs in the first year will be 60% of 100M equals 60M, then 60% of 500M equals 300M, then in the last year, 60% of 1BN equals 600M. Hence, my profits will be 100M-60M in the first year plus 500M-300M in the second year plus 1BN - 600M, which equals 640M of profits. Based on these calculations and considering the big assumption about our market share each year, our first condition will be met since 640M worth of profits will be generated in the first three years, greater than 500M, which is the initial investment.

Interviewer: Does this mean we should enter?

Candidate: Not yet. We must evaluate whether we have the skills to make such a move and the risks involved.

From a capital perspective, do we have the cash or the potential to take on debt to cover an investment of 500M and ongoing costs for the first three years? If we have the financial muscle, I don't think knowledge will be an issue since we can recruit experts to help us understand the market in detail and run our operations effectively.

Interview: Let's assume we have the budget

Candidate: We need to understand the risks from a business, operational, and regulatory point of view. In particular, I am worried about the last point: will the Chinese government allow a foreign entity to process all these payments? Where will they want the data to be stored? Isn't there the risk that they will implement some unfair competitive practice, supporting their national players against us?

Interviewer: The risk exists. Our main competitor opened its Chinese operations three years ago. They are now shutting down their operation because they realized that the Chinese government recently launched a new company with the same features and is the only one authorized to work with Chinese public entities.

Candidate: That's something we cannot ignore. Let's consider the potential risks associated with our business and operations.

From a business standpoint, we risk losing our investment if the government interferes. Additionally, the possibility of other Chinese companies copying our solution and features is significant. From an operational standpoint, the risk stems from the fact that a Chinese version of Stripe would require our servers to be located there and our engineering and operations team to be established there, among other things. Moreover, our platform must be adapted to fit the Chinese writing style. These changes could result in delays impacting our ability to break even within the designated time frame.

Interviewer: So, what are you telling me?

Candidate: From a financial perspective, it is undoubtedly appealing to consider entering this market. But the risks are too high. We might use many resources to enter this market and have to withdraw from it only a few years later. Hence, I would see if there are other markets that we could enter to grow our market share.

- **E: End with a bang.**

  Candidate: In summary, the main task was to evaluate whether Stripe should enter the Chinese market. I believe three conditions need to be met for this move to make sense:

  The profits generated by this investment need to cover the cost of the investment within the timeframe we have set.

  We need to have the skills to carry the project through to completion.

  The risks related to this initiative need to be manageable.

  Based on the assumption that we will be able to get 0.1% of the market share in the first year, 0.5% in the second, and 1% in the third, it looks like we would be able to generate a nice profit within three years, recovering all the initial investment of 500M. This condition may not be valid if our market share differs from what I assumed. Creating a worst-, medium-, and best-case for a more realistic view would be worth it. We then verified if we had the capital and the knowledge needed, and both aspects seemed fine. Finally, we considered the potential risks. There seem to be many risks here, and we wouldn't wholly control our fate should we embark on such an ambitious project. For this reason, we shouldn't enter this market of uncertainty as there is a high risk we might lose all our money without any possibility of fighting back.

- **"D: Don't forget to ask questions.** If this were the last question of your interview, now would be a great time to ask questions.

Chapter 10

TEN TIPS TO ACE ANY PANEL
(WITH A FEW ACTUAL CASE EXAMPLES)

"No one can label you a failure when what you are trying to do is audacious. Botching something easy is a failure. Failing in an attempt to achieve something huge is just courageous[27]."
—Anne Boden, CEO & Founder of the UK's first digital-only bank, Starling Bank

- You don't need to be in your 20ies to start your career in the tech sector. Anne Boden launched the first UK digital bank at 54. Let's see a few interesting facts about her remarkable career:

- Anne, a computer science and chemistry graduate, started her career at Lloyds Bank, where she contributed to the establishment of the UK's first real-time payments system. In 2012, she became the group chief operating officer at Allied Irish Banks in Dublin.

- However, at age 54, Anne took a bold step and launched her digital bank with the vision of offering customers a bureaucracy-free banking experience. Anne persevered despite many challenges, including male-dominated environments and accumulated debts

---

27 Forbes Magazine. (n.d.). Anne Boden. Forbes. https://www.forbes.com/profile/anne-boden/

exceeding £1m. After 8 months of sending emails to hundreds of contacts and potential investors, she secured financing of £48m from billionaire Harald McPike after a chance meeting in the Bahamas.

- The partnership with Tom Blomfield, initially a key figure in Starling's founding team, ultimately soured due to differences in vision and approach. Boden's willingness to prioritize Starling's success over personal pride led to her stepping aside and allowing Blomfield to take over the project, a decision she later reflected on with mixed emotions. Blomfield launched Monzo, one of Starling Bank's main competitors.

- Today, her digital bank, Starling, has over 1.8 million customer accounts, women occupy 40% of senior roles and employs over 1,000 staff. Read her book "Banking on It" to learn more about Anne's journey.

It's becoming increasingly frequent for companies to organize a panel interview as the last step of the hiring process. During a panel, you will be asked to present a deck in front of an audience of three or more interviewers, usually the stakeholders you will be working with most frequently. At Salesforce, for example, it's standard practice that every candidate goes through a one-hour panel in front of at least three different interviewers. The panel ensures you can present to an audience, answer unexpected questions, and express your thoughts.

Usually, you will be given a briefing, and it often looks like this:

1) Introduce yourself;

2) Share your view on the most critical trends in the industry;

3) Layout your strategy or vision for the role (with a 30, 60, 90-day plan);

4) Solve a role-related task or challenge;

5) Recap why you are the best candidate for the role.

Here are a few tips that can make or break your panel:

1. The day before the panel, **ask your recruiter to clarify what's expected, who will attend the panel, and the most common mistakes.** Ask if it's standard practice to have a pre-panel session with the hiring manager where you can share your doubts and remarks and gather additional details. If it is, take advantage of this opportunity and come prepared. Because the hiring manager is constantly evaluating you, your questions are as important as the answers you give! Ensure you have also researched information about the company and products sold. Use this information during the presentation. You must do your homework and understand what the company is selling and its competitive advantage.

2. **Connect on Linkedin with all the panelists before the panel**, introduce yourself, and thank them in advance for their time. It might seem trivial, but this shows proactivity, curiosity, and attention to detail. This will help you stand out and establish an initial relationship with your interviewers.

3. **Don't be boring!** Chances are you are the fourth or fifth panel these interviewers are going through this week. You need to think outside the box to stand out and keep their attention. You need to engage your audience! How do you do that? Ask questions during the interview, make the presentation personal, share information that is unique about yourself, play some games or trivia, and use pictures or videos rather than long texts or words. Prioritize your storytelling. As a rule of thumb, if you have been speaking for more than five minutes, chances are you have lost the attention of at least one of your interviewers (if not all). For example, you could use a slide of pictures of places you have been or your favorite dishes and ask each interviewee

about theirs. Then, you can link the picture to something interesting about your life or career. It's super easy to implement, but it will help keep the audience engaged and help you share details about yourself! Also, **avoid reading from a script at all costs.** You can jot down some notes to ensure you don't forget the essential points, but do not read from a script...it will make you lose all credibility and sound incredibly dull!

4. **Respect the time that you have been given!** If, in the panel's briefing, you are asked to present for forty minutes and to leave at least twenty minutes for Q&As, your presentation shouldn't last longer than forty minutes (not forty-one, not forty-three minutes)! Rehearse and ensure you can go through it without rushing the allotted time.

5. **Don't rush!** Speak calmly and clearly. You might be tempted to cover more content by speaking faster. But that would be counterproductive. Fewer, more explicit messages will be much more potent than a bunch of information shared quickly.

6. **Use pictures instead of long text, and make your presentation look great.** Long text in your slides should be avoided at all costs. It is difficult to read and doesn't add value, as no one will read a long paragraph anyway!

7. **Don't use acronyms or information that you cannot defend.** The last thing you want is for the interviewer to ask you for clarifying information on something you have written on the slide, and you don't know what it means.

8. **Use data and real-life examples to back up your statements.** If you are asked to develop 30, 60, and 90 days, avoid making this a theoretical exercise. Link your plan to what you did when you started your previous job

and showcase how your experience could help you hit the ground running in this next job[28]!

9. **Share your deck twenty-four hours in advance** with your recruiter (and your interviewers, if possible). That will give them a chance to review your deck in advance.

10. **Ask questions at the end of the panel**, but avoid asking about salary, financial conditions, or benefits. It is an opportunity to get to know your stakeholders: ask about them, what they do, and what they expect from this role!

Let's review a few real-life panel briefings from highly renowned tech companies. Due to confidentiality restrictions, we won't share the company's exact name.

---

28 To plan your first 90 days in a job, we highly recommend the book: *The First 90 Days: Proven Strategies for Getting Up to Speed Faster and Smarter*, Updated and Expanded, by Michael D. Watkins.

Sales Manager Panel - Top Market Research Firm

Prompt:

30/60/90 Day Plan Presentation (15-20 mins)

Task & Inputs: Create a presentation detailing your approach to the first 30, 60, or 90 days as a new leader within our team. Your role is to drive increased performance, create trust-based, value-added (TBVA) relationships with your people, and position your team and the business for success throughout the coming year.

Consider the following prompts when building your plan:

• How will I develop a strong culture of excellence and mentorship within my team?

• How will I drive increased sales productivity and performance?

• How will I gain credibility with my team, peers, and broader stakeholders?

• How will I connect with business partners and the greater team to ensure I hear our employees' and clients' most critical needs?

• How will I ensure my team gets off to a fast start?

Please use no more than three to five slides; you will have up to twenty minutes to present, and we will leave ten minutes for self-reflection/ feedback.

Give it a try: How would you approach this task? Which key concepts would you cover in your slides? How would you stand out from the crowd?

Leadership Position - Role-Play - S&P 500 Tech Company

Task: *As a leader, you will be expected to balance coaching, strategy, empathy, and execution at all times. In this section, you will be asked to role-play one of the scenarios below.*

Goal: *Showcase your approach to handling challenging situations and operating as a leader. Be prepared for standard objections; feel free to take liberties with the content. Plan to leave the conversation with a clear plan/ next steps. Timeframe: The role play will be approximately twenty minutes. We will leave ten minutes for self-reflection/feedback.*

Role Play #1

Scenario: An underperformer on the team feels they're doing the right things but cannot seem to hit their goals.

Context:

• *The Account Manager has been with the organization for two years.*

• *They sometimes hit their targets but struggle with consistency.*

• *You've identified that they consistently fall short of the minimum touch metrics and opportunity-creation expectations.*

• *The goal of this conversation is to diagnose the issues and produce an action plan.*

Allotted Time: Twenty minutes.

Role Play #2

Scenario: Your team's acquisition and revenue targets will increase at the end of the quarter. Your team has been consistently overperforming, and to ensure that the business continues to push the envelope on growth, the targets will become more challenging.

Context:

• *You are preparing for your bi-weekly team meeting, where you will deliver a message about your team's quarterly targets going up.*

• *You recently had a meeting with senior leadership where they told you the reasons for the change:*

• *To ensure the EOY forecast is increasing (the prior quarter's performance was exceptional).*

• *To ensure reps are being challenged.*

• *To ensure we continue pushing towards aggressive growth goals without necessarily adding headcount.*

Role-play how you will deliver that message and prepare to handle objections and questions from Account Managers on your team— allotted Time: Twenty minutes.

Account Executive Panel - FANG (Facebook/Meta), Amazon, Netflix, and Google/Alphabet)

Briefing: You are an Account Executive about to join the new business sales team selling a SaaS solution to public sector entities in Italy.

You have forty minutes to cover the following topics:

1. *Introduce yourself and explain why you are a good fit for the role.*

2. *Develop a go-to-market strategy, defining the top accounts you would be tackling and why.*

3. *Pick one of the accounts selected and tell us how you would pitch our solution to them.*

4. *Explain your 30/60/90 day plan in less than five minutes.*

Chapter 11

MASTERING SALARY NEGOTIATIONS

(SECURING YOUR WORTH)

"What is your desired salary? The unwritten rule regarding salary is this: whoever proposes a number first loses. When you interview, you should never feel pressured to answer this question. Simply let your interviewer know that the most important thing to you is how well you fit the position."

—Travis Bradberry is an award-winning coauthor of the worldwide best-selling book Emotional Intelligence 2.0 and the co-founder of TalentSmartEQ.

There are some valuable insights from the work of Dr. Travis Bradberry, who is an award-winning co-author of the highly popular book Emotional Intelligence 2.0. This book sold more than 3 million copies worldwide.

- One of the most important things to note is that when it comes to likability, people often focus on qualities under their control rather than innate characteristics like intelligence, attractiveness, or extraversion. These qualities include approachability, humility, and positivity. People who possess these skills not only tend to be highly likable but also tend to outperform others who don't have these skills significantly.

- Dr. Bradberry has identified several key behaviors that emotionally intelligent people engage in, making them likable. For instance, they tend to be genuine, which helps build trust. They also ask thoughtful questions and actively listen to people, which shows interest and helps build stronger relationships.

Additionally, they avoid being judgmental and are open-minded and flexible to other people's opinions.

• Another critical feature of likable people is that they don't seek attention. They are friendly, considerate, and recognize the contributions of others. They are also consistent in their behavior, which helps build trust. Finally, they use positive body language, greet people by name, and leave a solid first impression.

• In summary, emotionally intelligent people tend to be highly likable and successful because they possess qualities that people find attractive and engaging. Anyone can become likable and build stronger relationships by being genuine, asking thoughtful questions, avoiding judgment, being consistent, and using positive body language.

Well done! After hours of training, countless interviews, and a very tough panel, you were the top candidate chosen out of hundreds of applicants. You made it, and you deserve it!

It's time to see what your new employer can offer you…

Negotiating a salary is an art. It requires courage, confidence, and negotiation skills. Most people don't negotiate their salary because they fear losing the job offer they fought so hard to get. However, this is a false fear. **Career Builder research shows that 73% of employers will negotiate their initial offer[29].** When I hired Account Executives or Sales Reps at Google or Salesforce, I wanted them to negotiate their salary. If they didn't, that was an alarm bell as it meant they had no experience or inclination to lead a negotiation around money. And that's not a great start for a commercial profile. But that's not all. We often accept job conditions without understanding what they entail. It's typical for a sales rep to be offered a compensation package where 50% of the salary depends on achieving a specific

29 Hartley, D. (2022, October 13). 73% of employers would negotiate salary, 55% of workers don't ask. CareerBuilder's Employer Resource Center. https://resources.careerbuilder. com/news-research/73-of-employers-would-negotiate-salary-55-of-workers-don-t-ask

sales target. Still, the company does not indicate whether it is doable. It's standard to ask your employer for some guarantees! Hence, here are a few tips for negotiating your salary:

1) Once **you have passed the first phone screening** with the recruiter, asking for the salary range of the role you are applying for is wise. You want to save time for yourself and the hiring manager if the salary for the role is well below your expectations. However, refrain from negotiating during the screening phase: it might make you sound arrogant and only money-driven.

2) When asked for your current salary or salary requirements, try to avoid answering with a precise number; instead, give a range. You want to have some wiggle room for negotiation, so **always mention something above the salary you would like to get, including benefits.** But don't overshoot your current pay grade too much if you think that there is a chance that the recruiter will know you are bluffing. In that case, you will lose all credibility. You want to set the bar high but not too high. A good 25% to 30% above your current salary should work on average.

3) Wait until **you have passed all interviews, and they make you an offer before you negotiate your salary.** At this point, you have the highest bargaining power because the company has already invested quite a bit of time in you and because both the recruiter and the hiring manager see that they are very close to filling a role they (most likely) have been looking to fill for a while!

4) **You must give a detailed rationale if you ask them to revise the initial offer.** Why should you be paid more? It could be the existing network you bring, your years of seniority, the bonuses you will lose in your current role,

another company that made you a better offer, etc. There needs to be a reason for your request to be considered.

5) **Determine what you want from your negotiation and negotiate multiple benefits simultaneously.** Is it an increase of the base salary of 10k, a higher variable, a stock option, or more benefits? Jot down a list of what you want and tackle all the topics simultaneously. You want to avoid making one request at a time: "The base salary is too low. Can you increase it by 10k?" The new employer might accept your request, and then you realize your variables should also be higher. And so you ask for a second change to the contract, now an additional concession. If you had shared these asks simultaneously, it would have been easier to get them approved[30].

6) **Negotiating the offer by 5-10% is acceptable and expected.** Above that, it might be a stretch. There might be times when the employer says that the offer is nonnegotiable. In those cases, you might ask if some perks and benefits could be added at no cost to the employer, such as additional holiday days or more days working remotely.

7) **Don't focus just on salary; consider all the other perks and benefits.** Do they offer remote work? Do they allow for flexible working hours? If their salary is too low for you, can you compensate by asking them to provide some additional benefits (which will be tax-free for you!)? Here are some ideas:

   a) A later starting date (you might want to enjoy a period between jobs)

   b) Health insuranc

---

30 Check this great Harvard Business Review article for more ideas around negotiating an offer: https://hbr.org/2014/04/15-rules-for-negotiating-a-job-offer

c) Pension plan contribution[31]

d) A company car or a monthly car allowance

e) Additional days off

f) A wellness bonus for gyms or any other class that you might want to attend

g) A mobile phone or working-from-home kit

h) Stock options or shadow stock options in case the company is not listed yet[32]

i) A period of pass, several months in which you will be paid your full salary (fixed and bonus) regardless of your target achievement

j) A minimum number of guaranteed seniority years of seniority in case of an unjustified layoff[33]

k) A sign-on, one-off bonus

l) If you are changing countries, a relocation package includes flights for you and your family, relocation expenses, a house/apartment to stay in for the first few months, a relocation agency to support you in all the admin and help you find a new place to stay.

m) Restaurant gift cards

---

31 Google, for example, would allow employees to put up to 5% of their salary into a pension plan and Google would match that contribution so that the total money going into your pension plan will be 10% of your gross salary. This solution is interesting because it implies tax benefits for the company as well)

32 Usually, there will be a certain vesting period before you want to mature your stock. They will give you a certain amount, like $100K, vesting over four years. The longer you stay, the more stocks vest. You can negotiate on the vesting period.

33 This is particularly important if you are a senior person in your current company with many years working in that same company. You should not lose all that seniority by jumping into a new company that may fire you after one year if acquired or merged with another firm. You can ask them to recognize you at a certain number of years of seniority in case of these types of unjustified layoffs.

n) The possibility to attend a particular course or master's or MBA

o) A different job title

p) Days you can work from home every week/month

q) Paid maternity or paternity leave and childcare

8) **Always get everything in writing!** If they approve your conditions by phone, ask them to email you a recap of the new offer. "Verba volant, Scripta manent!"

9) Even if the offer sounds fantastic, wait twenty-four to forty-eight hours before accepting. Always think first, let it sink in, and consider whether the offer could be improved. You won't be able to negotiate once you have accepted it. When it feels right, go for it!

10) **Don't negotiate on an offer that you have not received.**

CONCLUSION

We want to share the last tip now that you have gotten this far. No matter how much you prepare or how good you are, fate will play a big part in determining the success of your interview process. Just accept it and embrace it. The manager's cousin might be applying for the same job, or the hiring manager might want someone who speaks German perfectly, even though it's unnecessary. Some things are out of your control and will play a crucial role in determining your chances of success. Accept it, and don't blame yourself if things don't go as planned. Does this make preparing for your interviews less critical? Not at all. The more you prepare, the more you train, and the higher the chances you will dominate the controllable aspects of your interviews. Remember that training doesn't mean just reading this book and trying a few cases online. The best way to train is to go through the interview process itself. List the companies you want to work for, from your favorite to the least favorite. Start by applying to your least favorites, and try to do as many interviews as possible before applying to the company and job you want the most.

The more interviews you do, the more relaxed and prepared you will be when you do the interviews for your dream job. That's just a fact.

Does it sound like a lot of work?

It is. But trust us, it is well worth it.

It will help you land the job of your dreams.

APPENDIX.

BASIC MATH YOU SHOULD KNOW

For most jobs in tech companies, you will not need to know complex math, but you will need to know basic math concepts. Below, we cover some of the basics and handy tricks that can save you time. Let's start from the basics:

x × 1 and x × 0	If you multiply any number by 1, the number remains the same. 10 × 1 = 10 5,000 × 1 = 5,000 If you multiply a number by 0, the result will always be 0. 10 × 0 = 0
x × 10 or x × 100 or x × 1,000	If you multiply any number by 10, you simply add a 0 to its end. 400 × 10 = 4,000 543,809 × 10 = 5,438,090 Similarly, if you need to calculate x × 100, you simply need to add as many 0's as there are in the 100 or 1,000. 30 × 1,000 = 30,000 400 × 10,000 = 4,000,000
x × 9	If you need to multiply a number times 9 (say 55 × 9), add 55 + 55 + 55 + etc. ... 9 times. The fastest way to calculate the results is 55 × 10 = 550 - (1 × 55)= 495.
99 × x	Let's try to figure out 99 × 100. The easiest way to do this is to multiply 100 × 100 and subtract 99. 100 × 100 = 10,000 10,000 - 99 = 9,901
x × 11	Repeat the same digit twice if you multiply any number up to 9 by 11. 4 × 11 = 44 8 × 11 = 88 If you need to multiply a number bigger than 9 by 11, you can multiply the number by 10, then add one more set of the number. 40 × 11 = 40 × 10 = 400, 400 + 40 = 440

x × 5	To multiply a number by 5, add a 0 to its end and divide it in half. 50 × 5 = 500 2 = 250
10% of x or 1% of x	Imagine that every number has a period to its right. Whenever you want to know 10% of a number, you simply move the period (called the decimal) one space to the left. 10% × 100 = 10% × 100.0 = 10.00 = 10 10% × 4,000 = 10% × 4,000.0 =400.00 = 400 10% × 35 = 3.5 10% × 57 = 5.7 If you want to calculate 1%, you will move the decimal two times to the left. 1% × 100 = 1 1% × 50 = 0.5 1% × 7 = 0.07
20%, 30%, or 40% of x	To get 20%, calculate 10% of the number and then multiply it by 2. 30% × 300 = 10% × 300 = 30 Then 30 × 3 = 90
5% of x	If you want to find 5% of a number, you find 10% and divide the result by half. 5% × 5,000,000 = 10% × 5,000,000 = 500,000 ÷ 2 = 250,000
2% of x	Simply find 1% and multiply by 2. 2% × 45 => (1% × 45 =) 4,5 *2 = 9
Learn these fractions by heart!	
1/2	½ = 0.5 = 50%
1/3	⅓ = 0.33= 33%
1/4	¼ = 0.25 = 25%

1/5	$\frac{1}{5} = 0.2 = 20\%$
1/6	$\frac{1}{6} = 0.16666 = 16\%$
1/7	$1/7 = 0.1428 = 14\%$
1/8	$\frac{1}{8} = 0.125 = 12.5\%$
1/9	$1/9 = 0.1111 = 11\%$
How to add quickly	53 + 34 You always need to simplify: 53 + 30 = 83 + 4 = 87. Let's try one that requires you to carry a number: 77 + 28. Simplify by breaking it into 77 + 20 = 97 + 8 = 105. If the number is composed of 3 digits, the strategy is the same. 539 + 425 = 539 + 400 = 939 + 20 = 959 + 5 = 964
How to subtract quickly	Let's say you need to calculate 1,563 - 587. Try to round the number you are subtracting 1563 - 590 = 973. Since we rounded away the 3, the final number is 973 + 3 = 976.

How to do proportions	Proportions are very useful, and they are used to say that two pairs of numbers (a,b & c,d) have the same ratio. It doesn't matter what the value of a, b, c, and d is. The important thing is that a:b = c:d

Let's imagine that the UK has 60% of the population driving a car (a). The UK population is 60M (b). Let's imagine the interviewer tells you that Italy has the same proportion of people driving a car (c), but with a population of 50M (d). How would you find the exact number of people that drive a car in Italy? Through a proportion.

$60\% : 60M = c : 50M$

To solve this proportion, you just need to multiply the two extremes (60% × 50M = 30M) and then divide the result by 60M = 50%.

If the proportion was like this 60M : 60% = 50M : c, with the variable at one extreme. Then you multiply the two central values (60% × 50M) and divide them by the other known number (60M). Hence:

$(60\% \times 50M) \div 60M = c$ |
| **How to divide quickly?** | There are multiple methods that you can use to divide quickly.

If you have to divide by 5, just multiply the number you want to divide by two, then divide it by 10.

$40 \div 5 =$
$40 \times *2 =$
$80 \div 10 = 8$

Another trick you can use is to try to divide by 2. This works especially well if the numbers are even.

$96 \div 4$ can be simplified to $48 \div 2 = 24$.

You can round the nominator to an even number if they are not even.

To understand if a number can be divided by 3, add all the digits in the number and find out the sum. If the sum is divisible by 3, so is the number. |

100 INTERVIEW QUESTIONS
TO PRACTICE

PERSONAL EXPERIENCE:

1. What have you done previously that fits the role you are applying for?

2. What added value could you bring to the company, and how would that positively impact the team?

3. Why do you want to apply to this role?

4. Why do you consider yourself a good match? Why should we hire you? Which products are you most interested in?

5. What are the most valued attributes for being successful in this job?

6. Give me an example of leadership.

7. What are the most significant structural or strategic changes you've dealt with in your career?

8. What is the most important project you have led? How did you track the success of the initiative? Looking back, what could you have done better?

9. What do you value when working in a team?

10. What are you looking for in your next career step and overall career trajectory?

11. What are your greatest strengths and weaknesses?

12. Can you give an example of a time when you managed a difficult client and how you handled the situation?

13. Describe a time you used your creativity to solve a problem or overcome an obstacle at work.

14. What skills or qualities are essential for success in a commercial role, and how have you demonstrated these skills in the past?

15. Tell me about a time when you had to use data or analytics to inform a business decision. What was the outcome?

16. What strategies have you used to increase customer retention and satisfaction?

17. Describe a successful sales campaign or project you spearheaded. What factors contributed to its success?

18. Provide an example of when you identified an untapped market opportunity. How did you capitalize on it?

19. What experience do you have working with cross-functional teams, and how do you effectively collaborate with colleagues from different departments or backgrounds?

20. Tell me of a time when you had to give negative feedback to a team member or colleague. How did you do it?

BEHAVIORAL

21. Give me an example of how you dealt with an issue with your team.

22. Tell me about a difficult decision you've had to make at work or school and the results of the decision.

23. How would you tackle an issue with your manager?

24. What is your approach to working with demanding colleagues?

25. How do you handle failure in the workplace?

26. How do you handle uncertainty in a project?

27. How do you handle challenging situations with clients?

28. Describe a time when you had to make a tough decision without all the necessary information.

29. Tell me about a time when you solved a complex problem.

30. Tell me about a time when you had to make a difficult decision about sales or client management.

31. How do you stay up-to-date on industry trends and changes? What impact do you think these trends will have on the commercial landscape?

32. How do you prioritize and manage a workload of multiple projects or clients?

33. How do you build and maintain strong relationships with clients and partners?

34. How do you measure the success of your sales and marketing efforts? What metrics do you use?

35. How do you approach market segmentation? What criteria do you use to identify customer groups?

36. How do you tailor your communication style to different audiences or stakeholders?

37. How do you stay organized and keep track of sales opportunities and leads?

38. How do you ensure your sales and marketing efforts align with business goals and objectives?

39. Tell me about a time when you made a mistake at work. How did you handle it?

40. Imagine your manager gives you too much work, and you realize completing everything in time will not be possible. What would you do?

GCA

41. How would you structure a $1M marketing campaign?

42. What is your favorite cafe? How much revenue does this shop make daily?

43. In the elevator, you meet the CMO of a large bank, who is skeptical about online marketing and spends heavily on offline media. You have one minute to pitch how TikTok and online marketing can increase his/her business success! Go!

44. You finally get to present to your CMO: what tools, analysis, research, and arguments would you use to convince this skeptical decision-maker?

45. What product would you change at TikTok/Google/etc.? Why?

46. What questions would you ask a client to qualify if they will be a significant revenue driver?

47. What would you do if you were behind quota?

48. How do you think you will be evaluated at TikTok?

49. Which strategies will you implement to increase our customer base?

50. How would you explain a database to a five-year-old?

51. How many golf balls can fit in a school bus?

52. How do you prioritize competing tasks?

53. You are in charge of a customer support team for product X. Usually, there are 50 complaints daily. Today, you arrive at work and notice there are 3,000 complaints. How would you resolve this situation? What additional information would you gather?

54. Imagine a large subset of employees at your company petitioning for a new policy allowing employees to work remotely. How would you analyze this proposal?

55. Imagine you receive an allegation that one of your employees is committing fraud by colluding with a vendor. How would you investigate this accusation?

56. Imagine you have to find the location for your company's new regional office. Walk me through the steps you would take to develop a proposal.

57. You are writing a document that team members worldwide will review. How would you ensure that team members from various cultural backgrounds understand your message?

58. You have bmet or surpassedyour yearly revenue targets for the past five years. This year, you are noticing a decline in sales. What would you do to find the cause of this decline?

59. You need to develop a set of rules to regulate a team of sales reps. How would you tackle this task?

60. You have been asked to set up a startup's hiring process to double the size of its current team of fifty people. How would you approach this task?

CONSULTING

Market Sizing

61. How many gas stations are in London?

62. How many planes depart from Ciampino Airport every day?

63. How many bottles of wine are consumed in a week in Europe?

64. How many light bulbs are produced in a year?

65. How many iPhones were sold globally last year?

66. How many sales could you generate in the first year if you were starting a fashion brand for kids?

67. What is the potential market size for a new electric car battery that lasts twice as long as the current batteries?

68. Estimate the size of the hair transplant industry in Turkey.

69. Estimate how many Mac computers are sold globally every year.

70. Estimate how many buses are active every day in the city of London.

Go/No-Go

71. You are the head of Apple's strategy department. The CEO asks whether it would make sense for Apple to enter the car industry. How would you determine whether it would make sense?

72. You are the CEO of Meta. A new startup has developed a quickly growing app similar to Instagram. Would you consider buying them out?

73. You are managing a team of Account Executives. Your manager asks whether you want to attend an event to acquire new customers in a new market. Should you attend the event?

74. Your friend recently launched a startup that is developing an AI tool. Should you drop your current job to join them?

75. You work for Airbnb. Your manager asks you whether you should enter the luxury goods vertical by starting to produce high-quality silk bed sheets. What do you say?

76. Your manager is considering publishing a book about digital marketing. He wants your help deciding whether to quit his day job to focus on writing books.

77. Our private equity client is considering purchasing a small company that makes mobile fitness apps. Sales last year were $50M, net profit was $20M, and the company has been growing at 50% yearly. What would you suggest?

78. I have just retired, and a great bed and breakfast near Lisbon's beach is up for sale. Should I buy it? Can you help me make this investment decision?

79. Apple is considering buying a small startup creating mobile phones from recycled materials for $300M. Should they complete the purchase?

80. Snapchat's stock price has been plummeting. The CEO is considering laying off 10% of the workforce and would like your help making a decision. What would you suggest?

Diagnostic

81. You are working for Revolut in France. While the number of subscribers is increasing, profits are plummeting. What's happening?

82. You recently joined the BDR team at Salesforce. Your managers asked you to develop an analysis of the team's previous results because it seems that the team is not giving a positive ROI. How would you conduct such an analysis?

83. The Christmas season is over. You are asked to analyze Etsy's sales. You notice that sales have been flat Year over Year, but profits have been growing. What's happening?

84. You own a small clothing shop in the center of London. Your rent just increased by 10%. How will this impact your profits next year?

85. The UN launched a program to incentivize microlending in Afghanistan and invested more than 100M in it. How can you determine whether it has been a success or not?

86. Google Search revenue has been dropping since the launch of ChatGPT. Investigate what's happening and suggest possible solutions.

87. Amazon has seen a profit reduction in its cloud department in the last two years. Help us understand what's happening.

88. You are the Head of Strategy of a video streaming platform called Netflix. Netflow has been investing millions in creating an original TV series, but the number of subscribers hasn't grown more than 5% in the last two years. What's happening?

89. You have recently opened a cinema in the center of your hometown. After two good years, your sales are declining, and you are running out of liquidity. What's happening?

90. Penco is a leading global manufacturer of writing products, with divisions in North America, Europe, and Southeast Asia. Penco's global sales equal €50M, whereas its profits are €25M. The major activities of Penco's European division are the manufacturing and sales of disposable pens. Within the European region, sales are flattening, and profits are decreasing. Penco's CEO has asked you to determine the cause of the decreasing profit in the European pen division and make suggestions to increase the profits.

Brainstorming

91. What else can you do to push sales up at N26?

92. Google has reached 90% market share in the US. Is there anything they can do to achieve 100%?

93. What would you do to reduce the illiteracy rate in India?

94. We have been contracted by a client who operates five domestic call centers throughout the United States. The company is considering consolidating its offices into a single location. How would you advise them?

95. Your client is a well-known contact lens provider called Contacto. Contacto manufactures and distributes contact lenses in the US. Contacto has been one of the most prominent players in the US market. However, the company feels it is not doing as well as it could compared to its main competitor. Contacto has called you to find out how to solve this problem and to recommend a solution.

96. The national revenue authority of an emerging country has hired consultants to improve the national tax income. The goal is to grow income by three times over ten years. What would you consider to help the client think through the issue?

97. A major retailer of clothing and household products has been experiencing sluggish growth and lower-than-expected profits over the last few years. The CEO has hired you to help her increase the company's annual growth rate and profitability. How would you do it?

98. Google Cloud has been growing quickly, but it's still far behind Amazon Web Services (Amazon's cloud product). What else can Google do to gain additional market share?

99. After five years of research and development, Apple has just launched a new watch. However, due to a lawsuit for patent violation, Apple had to withdraw the product after only two weeks on the market. What can they do to solve this situation?

100. You have a meeting with Tesla's Head of Product. You are expected to present an idea for launching a new product in the coming months. Which product would you propose?

ABOUT THE AUTHORS

Matteo Tonarelli is an Italian professional who has dedicated his life to creating and leading top-performing teams. After completing his Master's at Bocconi University and an MBA at the Université de Geneve, he worked with several startups in Germany, Nigeria, and Malaysia. Google (now Alphabet) came next, where Tonarelli filled various roles, such as Head of New Business Iberia and EMEA Manager for YouTube Partner Operations. He moved on to Salesforce, where he worked for two years as Regional Vice President, managing the Southern European Enterprise Corporate Sales team. He works as Global Vice President - Indirect Channel and Strategic Alliances at Odilo, EMEA's most prominent ed-tech scale-up. He has interviewed more than 500 candidates during his career, having built multiple teams and operations from scratch.

Pilar Alfonso Rico is a Spanish professional who has navigated her career across various countries, including Germany, the USA, Nigeria, Mexico, Oman, and Ireland. Her academic journey began in Law and Journalism and continued with an MBA. In 2016, she joined Google, where she served as a Business Development Manager. Her international exposure and commitment to technical excellence led her back to Spain, where she embraced a more technical role at META. Specializing in digital marketing consultancy and sales, Pilar has built her expertise. She paved the way for her next venture at TikTok, where Pilar is now Iberia's Head of Startups and VCs.